Emma Davenport, John Absolon

Fickle Flora and her Seaside Friends

Emma Davenport, John Absolon

Fickle Flora and her Seaside Friends

ISBN/EAN: 9783741144196

Manufactured in Europe, USA, Canada, Australia, Japa

Cover: Foto ©Andreas Hilbeck / pixelio.de

Manufactured and distributed by brebook publishing software (www.brebook.com)

Emma Davenport, John Absolon

Fickle Flora and her Seaside Friends

THE YOUNG FRIENDS IN THE ARBOUR.—*Page* 14.

FICKLE FLORA

AND

HER SEASIDE FRIENDS

BY

EMMA DAVENPORT

AUTHOR OF 'LIVE TOYS,' ETC.

Illustrated by John Absolon

GRIFFITH, FARRAN, OKEDEN & WELSH
SUCCESSORS TO NEWBERY AND HARRIS
CORNER OF ST PAUL'S CHURCHYARD, LONDON.

FICKLE FLORA;

OR,

THE TRIAL OF FRIENDSHIP.

CHAPTER I.

FLORA and CAROLINE were two little girls whose homes were very near together. They had been playfellows and companions all their lives; both were only children, both were taught at home by their own mammas, and they considered each other almost as sisters. Flora was about half a-year older than Caroline, and the most lively and vivacious of the two; but both were affectionate and good tempered, and enjoyed each other's friendship extremely.

The grounds of their pretty homes were adjoining. The house belonging to Flora's father was on rather higher ground than that where Caroline lived, and

Flora could see the chimneys and upper windows of the latter rising from the trees which surrounded it, close by the lodge of her father's park. A little gate opened into the park from the other garden, and when Flora saw the active little form of her friend bound through this little gate, she ran down across the park to meet her. If anything prevented Caroline from coming out at the usual time she hung out a white flag from her own room window, and this was understood by Flora to mean, 'I cannot come to-day.' A blue flag meant, 'Will you come into our garden?' and other colours, striped and varied, meant all sorts of different sentences; for contriving these signals had been a very great amusement to them, and on rainy days they could quite carry on a dialogue. At the happy hour of twelve their lessons ceased, and they usually ran out to play together. One morning, an unusual haste to reach each other was displayed. Caroline hurried through the little gate, and Flora rushed down the park so quickly, that when they had grasped each other's hands, they could scarcely speak for want of breath. At last, panting, Flora exclaimed, 'What do you think, I have some news!'

'So have I,' returned Caroline. 'I am not sure if I like mine.'

'But I like mine,' cried Flora. 'Guess! Oh! you will never guess it rightly; we are going away from home.'

'Why, so are we,' said Caroline. 'That is what I did not like: to leave you! Do you like to leave me?'

'No! but still I like to go; and if you are going too, you know nobody will be left?'

'That is true,' returned Caroline; 'but where are you going?'

'We are going to the seaside.'

'So are we!'

'To Scarborough?'

'Yes! to Scarborough!'

'How very odd,' exclaimed Caroline, laughing; 'but I daresay our mammas fixed on the same place on purpose that we might still be together.'

'Very likely,' returned Flora, 'especially as they are almost as fond of being together as we are. I am very glad! oh, so glad! I do not remember ever being at the seaside.'

'Now that I know you are going too,' said Caroline more quietly, 'I think I shall like it too, for I have never been at the seaside; but still there are many things which make me sorry to leave home!'

'What things?' asked Flora.

'Our gardens, for one thing, just as the summer is coming on, and all the plants budding and growing, the roses so beautiful, and all the annual seeds coming up so nicely!'

'Well, to be sure we shall miss seeing them, but we shall have all sorts of other things instead.'

'Yes, new things!' returned Caroline; 'but I do not know yet whether they will make up to me for my dear plants.'

'Oh, yes! I think they will,' said Flora. 'We have pretty much the same flowers every year; they are very nice, and I love them too, especially those that we planted ourselves; but I think I can be quite happy without them for one summer. And what else, Caroline, makes you sorry to go?'

'Why, my pony and my ring-doves.'

'Oh, Caroline! they will all be taken care of. Your Selim will have a good long run in the park, and the doves, I daresay, will scarcely miss you.'

'But I think they will,' said Caroline smiling; 'they coo, and look so pleased when I take them their food in the morning. Nice little soft things, *I* shall miss *them* at any rate!'

'I do not think I shall much miss my pigeons,' replied Flora; 'they are very tame. Do you know the fantails come to my window every morning, and I let them in, and they hop about the room; but I have had them a long time, and I am a little tired of them.'

'Oh, Flora, how can you say so! I am fonder of creatures and things of all sorts the longer I have them. But here we are at the paddock gate; let us look at your pony.'

Whilst the little girls were talking, they had strolled

along the plantation which skirted the park, until they came to a gate which led into the small meadow particularly appropriated to Flora's pony. It was a beautiful little black creature, without a speck of white, very glossy, and tolerably quiet; but Flora was a fearless and a good rider, and did not dislike a little prancing and liveliness. When Snowdrop's young mistress went to pay him a visit in the field, he came, arching his neck, and rubbing his ears against her, and if she ran about searching for wild flowers, he would follow her closely. The meadow was a most luxurious little spot, the hedgerow on one side was studded with trees, which gave a pleasant shade, and beneath them meandered a clear pebbly stream, in which the little girls caught many minnows. Dragonflies fluttered over it, and numerous lovely wild flowers grew on its edge.

'How pretty this field is,' said Caroline, as they sauntered along the stream, with Snowdrop following them, now and then thrusting his nose into Flora's hand, or over her shoulder; 'I doubt whether we shall see any spot so lovely at Scarborough.'

'Perhaps not,' said Flora, 'but it will be new, and though this is the dearest little pony in the world, and this the pleasantest paddock, I think I shall enjoy them all the more for a little absence. Don't you feel, Caroline, as if you would like to get away sometimes from everything and everybody that you always are with—in fact, that you want a little change?'

'No! I cannot say that I ever felt so; I think I would rather stay always and constantly at my own home, than go away or leave anything that I am used to.'

'Do you know what day you are to go?' asked Flora.

'Mamma said on Tuesday, and this is Saturday,' replied Caroline.

'And we go also on Tuesday. Oh! I am sure we shall enjoy it extremely; we shall bathe, and shall have an aquarium, and we shall hear a good band every evening in the garden, and perhaps go to some concerts, and drive about the country.'

'Shall we do our lessons there, I wonder?' said Caroline.

'I should think so, certainly. Six weeks would be a long time to learn nothing.'

'But we shall learn something about sea-shore things whilst we are there. Shall you not like that, Flora? There are shells, and sea-weeds, and sea anemones, and all kinds of beautiful living things on the sea-shore, and we know nothing at all about them.'

'Yes,' replied Flora, 'we can learn about them, and make collections, but that will be only for out of doors, and will do instead of our gardens and our pets. You know we could not be all the morning drying sea-weeds, and really I should miss my lesson hours very much, and I think you would.'

'No,' replied Caroline, 'I do not heartily like all my lessons as you do, they are more difficult to me. It is real work for me to learn by heart, whilst you can remember a verb, or twenty lines of verse, by once or twice reading over.'

'I know that I learn more quickly than you; but don't you remember, Caroline, what my mamma said when you stayed with us that fortnight, and did your lessons with me?'

'No! what did she say? I remember that I was dreadfully ashamed of keeping her so long waiting for me to say my lessons, when you had rattled yours off in a few minutes.'

'She said, "My Flora is the pleasantest pupil during the week, but when repetition day comes, give me Caroline; for she remembers what she has patiently and earnestly stored up in her little head, whilst Flora's knowledge has fled as fast as it entered."'

'Did she say so?' exclaimed Caroline; 'I am so glad that she thought me satisfactory in one way at least. But you see she noticed that I had to be very patient and earnest to learn at all. It is a trouble to me, and I think I should like a downright holiday and rest.'

As they talked they had gone quite round the meadow, and came again to the gate.

'Now we must go in to dinner,' said Flora, 'and

then I can come out again. Where shall we go this afternoon?'

'I am afraid I cannot go anywhere this afternoon,' said Caroline, 'or if I do it must only be for one hour.'

'Why! surely you can stay out till five as usual, can you not?' asked Flora.

'Not to-day,' Caroline replied, 'because I was very slow this morning, and had no time left for my work, so mamma desired that I should do it this afternoon.'

'Oh! this beautiful day!' cried Flora; 'to be shut up in the house with that stupid needlework; but, however, you will come out first;' and she ran off to her own home.

In about an hour's time the two little girls met again in the park.

'Caroline,' said Flora, 'I should particularly like to walk across the common this afternoon; cannot you hurry up your work after tea, or when you go to bed? Most likely your mamma only meant—"Have it done some time to-day."'

'But she *said* do it this afternoon!'

'Why, Caroline, I shall indeed call you Old Particular,' said Flora, laughing; 'but come, I will not try to make you idle and disobedient! May you take your work into your own arbour?'

'Oh yes, I may,' replied Caroline. 'Will you sit with me there?—that will be very kind.'

'I will help you to do your work,' said Flora, 'and then you will be rid of it in half the time.'

'Thank you,' said Caroline, looking rather grave; 'but I believe I ought to do all mine myself! Will you bring some of your own work?'

'Particular again,' exclaimed Flora. 'Now, do you really suppose that your mamma cares whether you do every stitch of that work yourself? I do not wish to persuade you wrongly, but I often think you are too fussy about the actual words that people say. Now you were a little idle this morning, and, as a punishment, your mamma said, "Do your work this afternoon." Surely if you are sitting at it for half-an-hour, that will answer all her purpose?'

'I never like to suppose that mamma means anything but what she says,' replied Caroline; 'and I remember so well something that she said when I was a very little girl!'

'That is so like you,' interrupted Flora. 'I wonder whether you remember all the nonsense that I say?'

'I do not recollect nonsense that anybody says,' returned Caroline, 'only particular things that are gravely said to myself!'

'What was it, then, that your mamma said?'

'Why, she was going out of the drawing-room, and I was playing on the floor, and she said to me,—"Do not touch the canaries' cage," and I went on playing for some time without even looking at the cage. But when I looked, I saw that the door was open; so I thought—"Surely mamma does not know that the door is open, and I had better shut it!" and I never noticed that one canary only was inside, and the other gone out. Presently mamma came in again, and at the same moment a canary came in at the window, and flew to the cage. But I had shut the door, so he could not go in, and after fluttering against the wire once or twice, he again darted out of the window. Mamma looked at me, and I cried out—"O mamma! I did not know one bird was out, and I shut the door; I am so sorry! I thought you did not know it was open!" So mamma said,—"This shows you that little girls should do precisely as they are told to do, and not imagine that their own opinions are better than their mamma's. I knew that my second canary would not venture out of the cage, and also that his companion would return if the door were left open. Let me think for you, Caroline, whilst you are young." And since that time, Flora, I have always done exactly what I am told, whatever I think myself.'

'But, Caroline, if we never think at all for ourselves, we shall not know how to think by the time we are grown up, when we *must* depend on our own judgments.'

'I suppose by that time we shall have more sense, and be able to do so; besides you know, Flora, that already many things are quite trusted to ourselves to

CAROLINE AND HER MOTHER.—*Page* 10.

think about and decide upon. Will you wait for me here, whilst I run for my work?'

'I will fetch some for myself, and I daresay I shall be back first!' So Flora darted off towards her own home, and in a very short space of time both the little girls flew into the arbour that overlooked Caroline's garden.

'There! you see,' cried Flora, 'I am back as soon as you are, although I had much further to run!'

'Yes!' said Caroline, good humouredly, 'you do everything faster than I do—even running.'

'I suppose it is because I am taller and stronger,' said Flora, drawing herself up, and peeping over Caroline's head.

'Well, it is quite right that you should be six months taller than me,' said Caroline; 'but I must really set to work, or I shall not have finished in time.'

'Now tell me, Caroline,' said Flora, as they soberly settled themselves to work, 'what things are these which we are allowed to decide about for ourselves; I cannot even think of one!'

'Our gardens,' replied Caroline. 'We do just as we like with them; plant what we like, and make the borders and walks, and everything just as we like. Don't you remember that I drew the patterns of this garden myself, and the arbour too, and mamma said the carpenter was to make it the way I liked?'

Caroline's garden had been a grassy sort of recess

or open space in one of the shrubberies; the trees that skirted it were mostly lilacs and laburnums, and the spot looked so retired and pretty, that the previous year Caroline had begged her mamma to give it to her, and to let her make her own garden there. She had amused herself extremely, by inventing pretty shapes for the flower-beds, and then the gardener had helped her to dig them out from the sod, leaving the walks between the beds of soft fine grass. Then her mamma had made for her a broad gravel walk, which curved and twisted round the little domain, near to the belt of lilacs and laburnums, and she had given her a day's work from a carpenter for the purpose of building an arbour of boards and laths. The back and part of the sides were of closed boards, with a nice little bench running round the inside, and the front part was of crossed laths. Caroline had paved it herself with round pebbles, and painted the woodwork. And when so far was accomplished, there had been much pleasant occupation in planting seeds and slips, and training creepers to cover the little arbour. The garden was now very pretty and very neat, as Caroline always spent some part of the morning in weeding, tying up, and sweeping her domains; and she was allowed no help in keeping it in order, except the mowing of the grass.

The arbour in which they sate was pretty well covered with a climbing rose and a Virginian creeper.

Caroline had planted some honeysuckles, but they grew but slowly, and had not yet reached the top.

'I suppose,' said Flora, 'that your having taken so much trouble with your garden is the reason why you certainly enjoy it more than I do mine. You know mamma had mine made for me; it is very pretty certainly; quite as pretty as this, but it is kept in order for me: and if I do not go near it for a week, I find it just as nice as usual; so it is not my own work.'

'But, Flora, I thought you had agreed to manage your own garden entirely, when it was given to you. I remember the time very well; it was your last birthday; and your mamma made you a present of it, full of flowers, and a whole set of tools in the arbour.'

'I did agree to take care of it; and I really kept to my agreement for a long time—for some weeks at least; and then I was very busy with something else for a few days; and when I went again to my garden, it was full of weeds; and the rain had beaten down some of the flowers; and it looked so uncomfortable, that I put off setting it in order; and I think I did not go near it for a week or more!'

'That was a pity,' remarked Caroline; 'for, of course, the longer it was left, the more trouble it would give you.'

'So, at last,' continued Flora, 'I was walking with

mamma, and she said, "Let us go and look at your garden, Flora! I have not seen it for some time;" and I dared not say, "Do not go there to-day;" and I followed her, feeling very foolish, and saying nothing. Certainly, I expected to see quite a heap of weeds and untidiness, but, to my surprise, it was all quite as neat as on the day when it was given to me! So mamma looked quite pleased and she went into my arbour, and there were hanging on their nails all my tools so clean and bright! Then mamma said, "I am so much pleased, Flora, to find that you have not wearied of this amusement, and, as you have found a pleasure in it so long, I do trust that you will not throw it up, when its novelty is a little more passed."'

'Oh, Flora! how unhappy you must have felt, not having merited that praise.'

'So I did,' said Flora, 'and I could not think what to say, so, like a goose, I began to cry, and mamma was so much astonished, and I had to explain that I had not touched a single thing in my garden for two or three weeks, and that the last time I looked at it it was a perfect wilderness.'

'I suppose, then, Flora,' said Caroline, 'that the gardener had attended to it, thinking to please you?'

'Yes; we met him as we left the garden, and he asked mamma if he had not better continue to take care of my garden, as it seemed too hard work for me.'

'Was your mamma angry about it?'

'She said that she was very sorry to see that her present had failed in its object, for she had hoped it would teach me perseverance, and make me find a lasting pleasure in my own work.'

'And do you now work at it yourself?'

'Very seldom; I am tired of it, at least, it is such a great deal of trouble raking and weeding every day. The truth is, I don't much care about gardening.'

'I do, very much,' said Caroline eagerly, 'and I think I become fonder of it every day. I feel quite grieved now to leave all these roses and buds, and my patches of seeds, which will come up when I am not here to watch them, and my creepers, which grow so fast, and want constantly training.'

'Oh, you will soon leave off regretting these things when we arrive at Scarborough,' said Flora, rather impatiently; 'and now, Caroline, have you not worked enough? Let us fetch our bows and arrows and try shooting till we go in.'

'I should like to shoot, but I am afraid I must finish this first.'

'What common sort of thing are you making, Caroline?'

'It is a brown holland jacket for going out in summer, for gardening, and running about, and I daresay I shall find it very nice and cool by the seaside.'

'Have you made it all yourself?'

'Yes, this and three others, and cut it out myself, too. Mamma gave me a long piece of the stuff, and a paper pattern, and said I was to cut it into four jackets. Oh! what measuring and contriving I had before I could make it do for all four.'

'Now, Caroline, I wonder what can possibly be the use of making you do all that. My mamma is just the same, so you need not colour up, and imagine that I am reproaching Mrs Leslie, but where can be the use of our learning to do common sewing? We shall both have plenty of money. *You* will have much more than I shall, I heard papa say, and as we can always have a maid to do these things for us, or let them be made by dressmakers, I do not see any sense in learning to do a thing that we never shall do when we are grown up. Yesterday, for instance, mamma spent half-an-hour in showing me how to darn my own sock, with a great long needle, a nasty thing pricking my fingers dreadfully every minute, and I am sure it was only waste of her patience and of my temper, and waste of a sock, and a heap of cotton, for you never saw such a thing as the sock became.'

'As to the riches we are likely to possess,' replied Caroline, 'that is a terrible uncertainty. Think of "Les petits Emigrés." Those children had not only to do these sort of things for themselves, but to work at a trade in order to feed themselves.'

'Oh! the French Revolution; but events like that so very seldom happen, and if it came to such extremes as in that book, I think it would be real fun having to do all entirely for one's-self. I should rather like that, but I don't like living like a lady's child, and also being obliged to do common tiresome work.'

'Well, Flora, supposing we do not become poor emigrants, but remain rich ladies, we shall have to manage and order our own servants, and unless we know ourselves how to do things, we cannot show them.'

'You might as well say that we ought to know how to clean houses, and how to cook everything.'

'I daresay all grown-up ladies do know those things. I remember one new cook that we had, making some curry for papa, and he said the rice was very badly done, and the next day mamma went and showed the cook how to boil rice for curry; so she had learned it at some time in her life, and I daresay we shall.'

'Now I remember that I have heard mamma say, "This wanted more boiling or more soaking," so she knows too how things must be cooked. But it is very stupid of the cooks, Caroline; *they* ought to learn all those things, not *we*.'

'The best way, Flora, is to try to learn what we are told, without thinking whether it will be useful or not. I shall remember the canary, and let mamma judge for me!'

'But these stupid kind of things take up so much time,' replied Flora. 'I want to learn the harp, and often beg mamma to let me begin; then she says, I have so many common things yet to learn that the harp must be put off. What a long time we have spent here in this sewing, and how willingly I would have practised on the harp for that time. There is our bell!' she exclaimed, starting up. 'Only Sunday and one more day before we shall be off!' and, separating, each ran away to her own home.

There was so much to do on Monday in packing and arranging for the move, that Flora and Caroline could only exchange a signal flag or two, to say, 'Too busy;' 'Can't come;' 'Are you taking your music books?' and so on. Neither did they see each other on Tuesday morning. Flora's family started the earliest, and arrived during the afternoon at the lodgings in Scarborough. Flora was eager to take a run upon the shore that very moment, and was rather annoyed when her mother desired that her own particular little trunk should be unpacked, and her books, her music, her workbox, and all her own property, should be neatly arranged before she went out. With a little grumbling this was accomplished, and she had just finished placing her books on the table that her mamma had set apart for lessons in the corner of the drawing-room, when she heard a knock at the door, and Caroline sprang into the room.

'Oh! are you come?' cried Flora, clapping her hands; 'I was afraid you would not be here till evening.'

'We are not only here?' replied Caroline, 'but all my things are unpacked, and so I see are yours, and I am longing to go to the shore, and mamma is waiting for me below. Will you come?'

Flora's mamma said that she felt tired, and did not wish to go out that evening, so Flora ran off with her friend.

CHAPTER II.

THE lodgings of both parties were situated in a sort of square, on the top of the cliff that overlooks the south bay, and close to a curious bridge called the Spa Bridge. Towards this bridge they directed their steps. It is narrow, and only intended for foot passengers.

'Oh, mamma,' cried Caroline, 'what an immense height we are from the ground; it makes me quite giddy to look down.'

'It is, indeed, scarcely pleasant,' replied her

mamma, 'but the view from this bridge is so extensive and so lovely that we will stand here for a while, and look about; and if you do not turn your eyes directly below the bridge, you will not feel giddy.'

'This deep valley,' said Flora, 'looks almost as if it had been cut purposely; is it not curious that there should be just this hollow and the cliff continuing so high on both sides of it?'

'Do you not see, dear Flora, that there is a little stream below us, which here finds its way into the sea? That stream is the workman who has hollowed out this dell. You will see presently that the cliffs here are very soft and friable, and therefore easily worn away by water.'

'And then, mamma,' said Caroline, 'this bridge has been built in order to cross the dell more quickly.'

'Yes, when we go down to the terrace on the other side you shall taste the mineral water called the Spa; and as many people come to Scarborough purposely to drink that water, they must have found it very fatiguing to descend all those steps that you see leading down to the shore, and then to remount them. Now, by crossing this bridge we can arrive at the well by sloping paths, and without wading through all the loose sand you see down below.'

'I do not think the sea so pretty as I expected, mamma,' said Caroline; 'I thought it would be blue water covered with little white waves, coming close up to the land like the water of a lake; but I only see a great width of wet sand. Can we walk upon that? I should like to go down close to the edge of the water!'

Flora laughed. 'My idea of the sea, Caroline, was not like yours! I expected to see very deep, dark water, and steep cliffs going sharp down into it. I never thought of all this sand.'

'Did you never hear of the tides, either of you? one of the most curious of natural phenomena. You surely knew, Caroline, that the water of the sea rises and recedes at certain times?'

'Yes, mamma, but I did not consider how it would look. This, then, is low tide?'

'Yes; to-morrow you shall see it at the high tide, and you will admire it more then, I am sure. You see we are now in a bay. Do you know, Flora, on what sea we are now looking?'

'Oh yes, it is the North Sea, or the German Ocean.'

'And what country lies on the other side, opposite to us now?'

'Norway, mamma,' said Caroline. 'Only think, Flora, nothing between us and the land of bears, and fir trees, and fiords, and so on!'

'Nothing but this wide, open sea,' replied Flora. 'Oh, I admire it very much. I think it is very grand!'

'*I* think so, too, Flora,' said Mrs Leslie; 'the sea is always to me a very wonderful part of creation. Always moving and rolling on and on, round about the shores of the globe, and never infringing on the limits marked for it by a mysterious and marvellous power. This great mass of water flows to a certain point on this smooth sand, and there must stop, and then return to its depths.'

'Very wonderful, mamma! Pray let us watch it to-morrow as it stops and retreats. And now may we cross the bridge and go into the garden?'

So they went on into a pretty garden constructed on the steep slope of the cliff; the winding walks were supported by stone buttresses in the steepest parts; many rustic benches and arbours were interspersed among the shady walks, and the whole prettily planted with varieties of ferns and every kind of flower that will bear the sea air. They descended by degrees until they came out on a broad handsome walk, protected from the inroads of the waves by a strong sea wall and parapet.

'This is very nice, mamma,' exclaimed Caroline, running to the parapet to look over. 'Oh, we are close upon the sand here; it looks very dry and firm. Can we not go down?'

'We will go out by that gate at the further end of the walk, and return, if you like, by the shore.'

'What is in this large building?' asked Flora, pointing to the inner side of the walk.

'Those are the concert and ball rooms,' said Mrs Leslie; 'there are two very handsome concert rooms, and many people consider the music and the gaiety that goes on in those rooms the best part of a visit to Scarborough.'

'I should so much like to hear a good concert,' cried Flora, 'but still I intend to enjoy the sea-shore immensely.'

'Mamma, I am surprised to see so many flowers. I fancied that garden flowers would not grow by the sea-shore.'

'It is generally supposed that they do not flourish; but you see, here are scarlet geraniums, verbenas, and calceolarias flourishing extremely well. I have heard it said that the particles of sea salt that settle on the plants fill up the pores of the more delicate sorts, and so kill the plants; but I imagine it must be the rough wind that so frequently blows off the sea that injures flowers. These, you see, are very much protected from wind by this wall, and although they must often be well sprinkled with spray, and of course receive all the salt contained in the air, still have no sharp blasts to endure.'

'Oh! we have forgotten the mineral spring,' cried Flora; 'where is it?'

'It is at the other end of the walk,' said Mrs Leslie,

'we came down upon the terrace very near to it. But I forgot it at the time; and now we have come to the further end of the walk, we will leave it for another day. There is the gate, and we can go down on the shore.'

A little sloping road of stone soon brought them on the sand.

'How pleasant it is to walk upon,' said Flora, 'so smooth and cool. Oh, are you turning back to the town? Cannot we go on under those cliffs along the bay?'

'You know we came out late, we had better not walk further this evening; we can go as far as that southern point of the bay to-morrow, if you like.' So they turned their steps homewards.

'That is a fine large cliff, with the ruin upon it, mamma,' said Caroline, pointing to the promontory that forms the north shore of the bay.

'Yes, it is extremely picturesque; the ruin is one of our oldest Norman fortresses. We will walk up to the castle some day. And the old town looks very well, covering the slope from the top of the cliff down to the shore.'

'What! are all those ships? Is there a harbour?'

'Yes, a small and not efficient harbour. You can see the pier at the outer side and a small lighthouse. Altogether, it is a pretty scene.'

'Why do you call that the old town, mamma? Is there a new?'

'That is the original seaport and fishing town of Scarborough; all the terraces and squares, and streets above, have been entirely built during the last few years for the sake of visitors, and besides this bay there is another larger bay on the north side of the castle, and all along the cliff that overlooks that bay are more terraces and streets—quite another town.'

'Which bay is the prettiest, mamma?'

'I scarcely can say. I like the north bay very much; the sands there are beautiful, far better than on this side, and it is much quieter. There is no Spa there, nor concert-rooms, or garden, and consequently it is much less thronged with visitors. It is quite a matter of taste which you may prefer.'

'When we have seen the north bay, and the castle,' said Flora, 'and have been to this southern point, we shall have seen all there is to see, so then we can begin searching for sea-weeds, and sea anemones, and all those curious sort of things.'

'All is at present quite new to you, Flora,' said Mrs. Leslie smiling, 'and therefore most delightful.'

'Do you not, then, think those things interesting?' asked Flora.

'Indeed I do,' replied Mrs Leslie : 'the marvellous vegetable and animal productions of the sea-shore present a study of infinite variety and beauty. I did not mean to say that in reality these things are only interesting whilst new.'

'But you think that *I* very soon tire of any pursuit; certainly, I do like things best that are new. This walk for instance, I have enjoyed it a thousand times more that if we had been walking in our own park, because I know every step of that, and am tired of it, whilst this sea, and sand, and cliffs, and the whole thing, is quite new. Do you think it wrong to like new things?'

'No, dear Flora, very right and very desirable that people should appreciate new scenes, and should have new ideas awakened now and then by novelty. But I do not think it desirable that you should feel tired of your own home, merely because you know every step in it.'

'Oh, mamma,' cried Caroline, 'does not that sound odd? *I* like things better because they are old, and I have known them so long, and Flora dislikes them for the very same reasons.'

'It merely shows your different dispositions. Flora is the most volatile, and the quickest at taking in new impressions. You are much slower, and having once made a thing your own, you cling to it and love it.'

But I, too, love some things that are old to me. Caroline, for instance. I have had her for a companion ever since I can remember, but I am not tired of her.'

'Have any other companions ever been thrown in your way, Flora?'

'No, I think not, I do not remember any; but I am certain I should never feel tired of Caroline.'

'And I am sure that I shall never even *begin* to like any other girl,' said Caroline. 'I am so glad we both came to Scarborough; I should have been quite lonely here with only you, mamma.'

'That is very complimentary, Caroline,' said Mrs. Leslie, laughing; 'but I quite agree with you, that you would very much have wanted a playfellow younger than myself. Now, we must turn up here,' she said, as they came opposite the bridge.

'What an immense height it is,' exclaimed Flora; 'one can almost fancy it quite unsafe.'

'Those arches are seventy feet high,' said Mrs. Leslie. 'They are certainly very slight, but you must remember that no horse or carriage goes across, and the weight and the shaking caused by foot passengers is very small. The only part of it which appears to me insecure is this middle pier, which is placed in the reservoir where the stream is banked up, and it gives the idea that the foundation might be loosened by the water. But I suppose there may have been some good reason for so placing it.'

'It is very pretty,' said Caroline, 'to see the road and the trees through the bridge. What is that strangely-shaped round house a little way up the hill?'

'That is the museum. A great many curiosities

are arranged there, and a collection of stuffed birds and insects, and minerals. We shall go some day, perhaps often, to see it, when you are a little tired of the sea-shore. Now we go up these steps.'

As they were slowly mounting the steps, Flora asked whether Caroline was to have the same hours for her lessons as at home.

'Not quite, I think,' said Mrs. Leslie; 'I wish her to be out of doors a great deal whilst we are here. I should like her to have an hour's run on the shore before breakfast, and then to go out again till about eleven. During the heat of the day it will be best to remain in the house, and lessons can be done then. And afterwards shall we take a good walk in the cool of the evening?'

'Yes! how do you like that plan, Flora? Do you think your mamma would like you to have the same hours?'

'Yes, I think she would; for mamma is not a very good walker, and I can go out with Caroline. I am sure she will like it. So I shall ask her to let me go out and stay in just when Caroline does.'

'I daresay she will have no objection to your going out together in the mornings without me. You will keep to this bay, or remain in the Spa gardens, and in the evenings I shall generally be able to walk with you.'

'Then, Flora,' said Caroline, 'you will come on the

Spa bridge to-morrow morning at eight o'clock, if you have leave!' and so they parted.

Very beautiful on a calm summer morning is the sea-shore! The sparkling, heaving mass of live-looking water gives a sort of animation to the landscape that is wanting in a purely rural scene. So Caroline thought, as she leant against the side of the bridge waiting the arrival of her friend. The water was much higher than it had been the previous evening, and was falling on the sand in gentle little waves. There was a sort of hum rising from the distant pier, where a crowd of boatmen, fish vendors, women, and children were assembled. The castle cliff stood out clear and sharp against the blue sky, and the southern point of the bay looked so near and so distinct, that Caroline could scarcely imagine it to be two miles distant, as her mamma had said. She thought she could have remained there motionless all day; and, in fact, it must have been full half-an-hour before Flora's cheerful voice addressed her,—'Oh! you are here already, Caroline!'

'Indeed I have been here a long time,' returned Caroline; 'stay here a little while and admire this lovely view! How I should like to go smoothly across that wide sea till I began to see the opposite shore, very faint at first, and then by degrees perceiving trees, and houses, and fields, and people!'

'Yes,' returned Flora, 'it looks just now very bright

and pleasant; but I do not believe that we should in reality like a sea voyage at all!'

'No, perhaps not! but it is nice in imagination, at any rate, on such a morning as this.'

'I wonder whether we shall bathe?' said Flora. 'Look at the machines down there! how small the people look, and how curious, popping about in the water.'

'I should not at all like to bathe,' said Caroline, 'with so many people close about. Let us come into the garden, and then down to look at the well.'

There were a great number of people in the garden, and among them very many children.

'Oh! Caroline,' whispered Flora, 'look what pretty girls!—they seem about our age—and how prettily they are dressed!'

But Caroline had no eyes excepting for the sea, and the cliffs, and the blue sky.

'Did you notice them?' asked Flora, when they had passed.

'No, indeed, not much. I saw three girls and a lady, but I did not look at them particularly.'

'One was of my size, and one about yours, and a younger one. The eldest had beautiful curly hair and rosy cheeks, and the second was a darker girl with black eyes, and they looked so merry, and were beautifully dressed.'

'I should not like to be beautifully dressed here,'

said Caroline, 'I wish to go down by the waves, and to hunt for weeds and sea creatures, so the commoner clothes I wear here, the more comfortable I shall be.'

'I think I should like to know those girls,' said Flora. 'I wonder who they are?'

'*I* do not wish to know any girl but you, Flora,' replied Caroline; 'at any rate, whilst we are here, where there is so much to see and to do.'

'Where can that well be?' she continued, looking round as they stepped down on the terrace. 'I do not see anything in the least like a well.'

'There are some people going down those steps,' said Flora; 'perhaps they may lead to it.'

So they followed down the flight of steps, and found themselves in a sort of round court, walled and paved.

'Is the Spa well here?' asked Caroline of a woman who stood at the bottom of the steps.

'Yes, Miss,' she replied; 'the water runs from those two spouts; you can taste it, if you like.'

On each side of the circular court was a small fountain, or rather running pipe, and on a stone table in the middle were a number of glasses with long handles.

Flora took one of these, and held it under the pipe; then she tasted it.

'Why, it has scarcely any taste at all. It is fresh and cold—try, Caroline.'

'I think it tastes a little of iron,' said she, finishing

the glass, 'but it is not disagreeable; now, let us try the other.'

The second fountain had rather a stronger taste of iron.

'What is the water good for, I wonder?' said Caroline.

'I never heard,' replied Flora; 'happily for us, we are not sick, and do not need it. Now let us go on the sands for a little while. Oh, the tide is very high!'

'But there is still plenty of sand left to walk on. Come, Flora!'

'I suppose the tide is going down now. Do you see, Caroline, how wet all this sand is? There is the mark where the last wave has reached, and then stopped, as your mamma was saying, by some mysterious power. Let us go close to the edge of the waves; how pretty they are, rolling over so gently. I like the sea this morning much better than I did last night.'

'It looks nicer certainly when it is high up on the shore, but we shall only be able to find weeds, and shells, and zoophytes when the tide is low; then we can climb upon the rocks, and search about in the crannies for all sorts of curious things.'

'I think I should never be tired of watching these waves,' said Caroline, 'but I shall enjoy finding odd things. When shall we begin?'

'We must find out when the tide is low,' replied

FLORA AND CAROLINE ON THE SANDS—*Page* 34.

Flora; 'it was quite low last night when we came down here about six o'clock—I suppose it will be the same to-night?'

'Not quite the same, Flora; it is a little bit later every day, and the high tide, which is twice in twenty-four hours, is at intervals of twelve hours, so it will not have been quite so low yesterday at six, for you see it has only just turned back now, and it is scarcely nine.'

'No; then it must have been coming up last night when we saw it?'

'Yes; and would have been high about half-past eight, and was high this morning only a little later, to-morrow a little later still, and the next day later still.'

'But when will it be low?'

'Why, six hours from the time it is high—to-day about half-past two.'

'Well, we must wait until low tide, late in the afternoon; but, Caroline, how do you know about the tide? I did not.'

'I was asking papa about it last night, and he told me a little, that the rise and fall of tides are supposed to be caused by the attraction of the moon, and that their time varies according to the motion of the moon. But he said that it was a very difficult subject, and he thought I could not understand much more about it at present.'

'Well, we can at any rate make a pretty good guess about the times of high and low tide, and that is all we want. Had we not better go home now?'

'Yes, I am afraid we must go; I am quite sorry to leave this delightful shore.'

'By the time we go home again,' said Flora, laughing, 'you will have as many regrets for the waves as you had for the garden, and the birds, and all the things at home.'

'Not quite, I think,' replied Caroline; 'and you know we ought to make the most of the sea, as we only have it for a short time.'

'And now we must really run home,' said Flora; 'do you hear that clock striking?'

A busy morning followed, the time passed pleasantly to Flora, who at all times liked her lessons, and who, naturally volatile, could easily turn her mind from one subject to another. Not so bright to Caroline was her first day's study at Scarborough, for though desirous and eager to learn, she was so much impressed by the novelty and wonder of the mighty sea, that she could not prevent herself from dwelling on the idea, and pondering over it. Luckily her mother understood what passed in Caroline's mind, and knowing that her distracted attention was not the sign of an empty, idle, disposition, it was passed over with but little comment, and towards evening the two little girls met again in the square.

'Now, Mrs Leslie,' cried Flora, springing about from one side of the path to the other, 'where shall we go? There is the castle-hill, and there is Oliver's Mount, and the museum, and the point at the end of the bay.'

'And the north bay, on the other side of the castle,' said Caroline.

'I propose, then,' said Mrs Leslie, 'that we shall first go to the north bay, then we shall have a good idea of the position of the town and the castle promontory. Do you not like, Flora, when you go to a new place, to have a kind of map in your head of all the localities? I never feel myself quite comfortable anywhere until I know how we are placed on the globe—what is behind us, and what before us, and so on.'

'That sounds very odd,' said Flora laughing. 'I know geography very well, mamma says, but I never imagined myself standing on the world anywhere.'

'I think I *do* sometimes, mamma,' said Caroline. 'I like to think that far away over that sea lies Norway and Sweden, and more towards the north that there is nothing at all between us and the North Pole. Nothing, Flora, to prevent us feeling the air directly off the icebergs.'

'And what is behind us, Flora?' asked Mrs Leslie.

'Why, the land of Yorkshire, to be sure.'

'Yes,' said Caroline; 'but think of more than that,

the whole width of England behind us, before we come to any sea again!'

'And then?'

'Then the Irish Sea, then Ireland, and then another wide, wide ocean. It makes me feel like a fly, mamma—like an atom.'

'So we are atoms compared with oceans and lands, and then this beautiful coast, these cliffs and sands, with the sea bounding all, do not they lead you to think of their continuity all round our island?'

'Bays, and promontories, and sands, and waves, over and over, mamma, all down the eastern coast, then along the shore of the English Channel.'

'Then up again, along the coast of Wales,' said Flora.

'And then,' said Mrs Leslie, 'a wonderful variety of islands, and inlets, and gulfs, and seas, and rocky caverns all along the western coast of Scotland.'

'Then round the top of Scotland, mamma.'

'Yes, a most wild and extraordinary coast, craggy cliffs, such as you cannot conceive, rushing currents and eddies of the sea that are fearful!'

'Then, mamma,' said Caroline, 'we should return all down the east coast of Scotland.'

'Yes, a coast rich with relics of history and interesting spots; and then, again, come our quieter but beautiful English shores.'

'It would be very pleasant,' said Flora, 'to make

an expedition quite round England and Scotland, and to visit all the remarkable places, and to learn all about them.'

'To visit them all would indeed be very pleasant and amusing, but to learn all about them would, I doubt, be rather too much for your little heads.

'There would be all the history of each place,' said Caroline.

'And who first discovered or possessed it,' added Mrs Leslie. 'Whether savage Briton, or warlike Roman, or rude Saxon, or knightly Norman. Whether the site of the modern town was once the bottom of some ocean, or the now woody height perhaps in former ages a fierce desolating volcano.'

'And what plants and trees grow and flourish best in each place,' said Flora.

'And how the inhabitants now live, and trade, and thrive,' added Mrs Leslie.

'Oh! mamma,' cried Caroline, 'we should indeed have to content ourselves with learning just the chief things about the places on our coast journey.'

Whilst they were talking they had passed through the streets of the town, and now emerged again on the top of the cliff which overhangs the north bay.

'Here is a fine open view,' said Mrs Leslie; 'this bay is so much less confined than the southern side of the castle rock, that I think I prefer it.'

'But it is so much livelier on the other side,' said

Flora; 'so many people moving about, and the port, and the fishermen, and the bathing, make it much more amusing.'

'I acknowledge that this is much quieter, but I like to see that long expanse of shore, with the smooth unbroken sand, and then the castle cliff is much finer on this side, so steep and inaccessible. Which do *you* prefer, Caroline?'

'I did not know at first, mamma, and when Flora spoke so decidedly I thought *I* could not say distinctly what is my opinion. But now I know I should like to *live* on this side, with nothing but the wide sea and the quiet sand, and that grand cliff, and I should now and then go to the south bay for a time to see and enjoy all the bustle.'

'Well, then, you combine my taste and that of Flora,' said her mother, 'or rather the old and the young idea!'

Flora laughed. 'I always say, Caroline, that you are like an old woman! But I do not mean,' she added, colouring, 'that *you* are an old woman, Mrs Leslie.'

'Do not fear that I shall misinterpret you, Flora,' said Mrs Leslie; 'I know perfectly what you mean about Caroline; she is often a little bit steadier than yourself, but you see she has also a slight touch of your youth, and does not entirely approve of my quiet shore. Shall we go down?'

'Here are the steps,' cried Flora, rushing down the path; it was rather steep and rather muddy, being supported here and there by rude steps of wood. Flora had started with such impetus, that she soon found herself obliged to run as fast as possible; and towards the lower end it was as much as she could do to keep her feet.

Mrs Leslie and Caroline followed rather more slowly.

'Now, Mrs Leslie,' cried Flora, as they approached her, 'I am sure you cannot prefer this nasty, dirty, rough path to the stone steps and nice gravel walks in the Spa garden. I could have run down there quite pleasantly.'

'But, my dear Flora,' said Mrs Leslie, 'Caroline and I have come down quite pleasantly. Was it not your own will and pleasure to rush down the cliff like a wild bull.'

'Not exactly,' replied Flora; 'I did not begin running at quite such a rate: but now I will really enjoy these lovely sands; how smooth and fine they are!'

'I believe you may find some pretty pebbles here. If you take a littte trouble, there are carnelians, agates, and onyxes on this coast, I believe. Bring me several, and I will show you what kind of outsides they have.'

Many handfuls were brought, and Mrs Leslie at last

picked out three or four that shone transparently when held up to the light, and were of a yellowish or reddish colour. These, she thought, were carnelians. And a few that had a mottled whitish sort of outside were kept, as likely to prove agates; and in seeking these pebbles, and in watching the waves, they had wandered to some distance along the bay, and were surprised, on turning, to find at what a distance the castle cliff appeared.

'Come, my dear girls,' said Mrs Leslie, 'we must hurry home. Do not collect any more pebbles now. I will have these cut for you by a lapidary. It is a pretty process, and you shall see it done.'

'Which are the best kinds of pebbles, mamma?' asked Caroline.

'I can scarcely say,' replied Mrs Leslie. 'The carnelian, chalcedony, onyx, sardonyx, Mocha stone, and bloodstone are all varieties of agate, which is a very pure silica; and the varieties of colour are chiefly produced by minute infusions of iron.'

'And how are we to distinguish the different pebbles from each other?' asked Caroline.

'Carnelian is the commonest on this shore,' said Mrs Leslie; 'it is of one uniform colour, not striped or varied, it is either a shade of clear red or yellowish, and sometimes it is quite white. This sort is much used for seals, and formerly valuable designs were engraved upon it, that are now termed gems. Very large, handsome carnelians are found in Japan; what we have here are comparatively very small and poor.'

'Then, mamma, what is chalcedony like?'

'Chalcedony is so called because it was first found and valued at Calchedon, or Chalcedon in Bythynia. This is also uniform in colour, generally a pale muddy yellow, or whitish yellow. It is found in larger pieces than carnelian, but I do not think it half so pretty.'

'I know what onyx is like,' said Flora; 'papa has a large seal of it; it is striped white and brown.'

'Yes, and sometimes it is varied by bluish or grey stripes. This stone has been used for cutting cameos; it is coloured as you described, Flora, in stripes or layers. Now suppose a white layer at the top of the stone, a head or figure is sketched upon that, and all round the design, the white layer is cut away until the brown or grey layer beneath is reached, so that the figure appears raised in white upon a brown ground.'

'Oh! mamma has one of those carvings,' cried Flora; 'some beautiful little white figures standing out on a brown ground.'

'Your mamma's, I think, is one of the modern Roman cameos; they are cut in shell, and have just the same effect as the antique onyxes.'

'Then the sardonyx?' asked Caroline.

'That is a variety of onyx, with more yellow and a more beautiful colour in the brown stripe. I believe they are more rare, and therefore more valuable than the onyx. These two last are found in various parts of the shores of the Mediterranean, and I doubt whether good specimens are ever met with here.'

'I have seen a moss agate,' said Flora, 'which I thought very beautiful; it seemed to contain little branches of brown moss.'

'They were in reality bits of brown moss. I think myself that the moss agate is by far the prettiest of this class of pebble; it is very transparent chalcedony, varied by different infusions of coloured earths and iron, and often by the siliceous particles having enclosed during the progress of formation bits of moss, or sponge, sometimes coral, or madrepore; and sometimes even the clear crystal-looking stone has within it an actinia, or what people often call a zoophyte—one of those curious live flowers, which are among the beautiful wonders of the sea-shore.'

'Oh, mamma, I should so much like to find one of those creatures turned to stone!'

'I fear you will not find one here; they are numerous and large on our southern coast. I have seen them at Bognor, and at Hastings, and other places on the Sussex coast, and I have one or two at home. But you must content yourselves here with carnelians, and the smaller kinds of agates. Those fortification agates are very pretty, they have parallel white lines like the walls of a fortification, but I think that this kind should really be considered as small onxyes.'

'Do you know,' said Caroline, 'that there is a bay somewhere near here called Carnelian Bay.'

'Yes, it is beyond the southern point of the south bay; we will go there before we leave, and by searching well, we may chance to find larger pebbles than on this shore. And now we are approaching home, so we will say good-night to you, Flora, and may renew our search for pebbles to-morrow.'

'Perhaps we may find some good ones before you are up, mamma. Do not be late, Flora.'

CHAPTER III.

WHEN the little girls met next morning, Caroline was eager to go down to the shore, and to renew her search for pebbles, but Flora rather wished to linger about the walks of the Spa garden, in order that she might again see the little girls who had so taken her fancy.

'Do stay here, Caroline,' said she. 'It is far pleasanter here than on the shore with no shade from this hot sun.'

'But, Flora,' urged Caroline, 'do not you wish to find some more of those beautiful pebbles? I shall not be satisfied until I have one tolerably good specimen of each sort.'

'Each sort, Caroline! don't you remember that your mamma said only a few kinds were to be seen on these shores?'

'Yes! but I should like to find all that can be found, and perhaps we may go to a lapidary this afternoon to see them cut.'

'Well, but we already have several for the man to begin upon. Now do, Caroline, give up your shore and your pebbles this morning, and let us run up and down these shady pretty walks.'

Caroline gave way, saying, 'Very well, Flora, I shall stay here, as you wish it so much, but pray tell me your reason for preferring shady walks, which we certainly can have at home, to the sea-shore which we cannot have?'

'If you must know,' said Flora, smiling, 'it is that I wish again to meet those three pretty girls, and if I can describe them exactly to mamma, perhaps she will find out who they are, and will get acquainted with them. I quite long to know them.'

Caroline said nothing, but thought to herself, '*I* am quite contented and happy with Flora for a companion; but I am not sufficient for her, I suppose, and I am afraid that I must be a very dull girl.'

And the feeling that Flora considered her so, did not tend to make her more lively that morning; and at length, as they wandered up and down the walks, Flora remarked,—

'Come, Caroline, talk a little; you are unusually quiet this morning. What is the matter?'

'I felt sorry,' replied Caroline, 'that you should be so eager for other companions. *I* want nobody but you, and I suppose that you must find me very dull and stupid.'

'No! not at all, you silly girl,' said Flora, laughing. 'You are a very good companion, and I like you very much, but that is no reason why I should not also like others. You must not want to keep me all to yourself, Caroline, for, I assure you, I mean to have a great many friends when I grow up, and to make acquaintance with all the pleasant people I can find. So don't be jealous! There they are! I declare,' cried she; and she darted down to the walk below, into which the admired trio had just passed. Caroline followed slowly, but the three sisters were sauntering along at so slow a pace, that Caroline came up with Flora, who followed them at a little distance.

'I hope they will turn round soon,' whispered Flora; 'I want to have a good look at them.' And she had her wish, for at the upper end of the walk they turned, and came down again.

'Now, do look at them well,' again whispered Flora, as they approached. The three sisters seemed equally desirous to scrutinize Caroline and Flora, and as they passed closely by, they scanned them from head to foot.

D

'There,' said Flora, when they were out of hearing, 'they examined us as much as I examined them; I do hope that I shall know them. What do you think of them, Caroline?'

'I think they are very pretty, and, as you said the other day, beautifully dressed; but I thought they stared at us very rudely, and with a sort of smile that seemed quizzing.'

'Nonsense, Caroline!' replied Flora; 'why should they quiz *us*? We are not dressed so smartly as they are this morning, but we are altogether quite as nice looking. No! no! I daresay they noticed us, as being about their own age, and very likely wished that they could know us. I think the eldest is the pleasantest looking.'

'I thought the youngest was the gentlest looking, and not quite so well satisfied with herself as her sisters appear to be!'

'How sarcastic you are, Caroline,' said Flora, shaking off her friend's arm; 'they look very merry, and very nice, but *you* will not think so, because you do not wish me to like them as well as I like you.'

'Well,' said Caroline, smiling, 'I confess there is some truth in that; but take my arm again, and I will not be jealous of them, even if you do become great friends, because I hope that you will have sufficient love for me and them too.'

'Do not you mean to like them too, then?'

'No! I care nothing about knowing them, and do not want to have many friends.'

'You are an odd girl, Caroline! But come, have not you in your sober wisdom found out that we shall be late for breakfast, unless we run up? You see my steadiness, after all, is less disturbed than yours, by the idea of these beautiful girls. Come, now, quick!'

And they arrived at the end of the Spa bridge panting and out of breath.

'Which would you prefer this afternoon, children?' asked Mrs. Leslie, as they stood at the end of the bridge that afternoon. 'Shall we walk along the shore beneath the cliff, perhaps as far as that point; or shall we spend the afternoon in the museum?'

There was a little hesitation before they could decide.

'It is a lovely afternoon, mamma, for the shore,' said Caroline.

'But very hot,' added Flora; 'and I dare say it is cool and nice inside that museum.'

'Then we will manage this way,' said Mrs. Leslie; 'there is an aquarium, or case containing water for live marine productions, in the museum, we will just go in to look at that; and a little later in the afternoon, when the heat of the sun will be less, we can go a little way along the shore, and see if we can find anything similar.'

This was readily agreed to, and they turned their steps first to the museum, rather an ugly circular building not far from the Spa bridge. The entrance presented many objects which would have tempted the little girls to remain, but Mrs. Leslie said, 'Not to-day, Caroline; we came here with one object, and we will keep to that; do not contract a habit of being diverted from your purpose by the first thing that presents itself.'

'Now, dear Mrs. Leslie,' cried Flora, 'although you addressed that observation to Caroline, I feel sure that you almost meant it all for me, for really that is not one of Caroline's failings; but I fear it is one of mine. I know I like to fly off from whatever I am about, to the first amusing thing that comes in my way.'

'If you are conscious of such a failing, Flora,' replied Mrs. Leslie, 'there are hopes that you will determine to overcome it. But I fancy, sometimes, that you have a little affection for your own bad habits or faults, and rather cling to them than try to rid yourself of them. Is it not so?'

Flora blushed. 'Do you think that I am quite true and honest? I mean, that I really say what I think and believe?'

'Yes, indeed I do, Flora; that is one of your best traits.'

'Well, then, I shall tell you, that I do not try very much to mend that, and many other small faults; for after all it is but a small fault.'

'Before we talk of that especial fault, pray let me know why it is that you do not try to mend all small faults; or rather to throw them off from you altogether?'

'It is because I always think that very good, precise people are rather tiresome—even Caroline. Do not be vexed with me if I say that sometimes I wish she were less particular, less desirous to be always right and good; she would be more amusing to me, and we should have more fun.'

'And, dear Flora, do you truly imagine yourself to be so near perfection that, were you to improve in goodness, you would frighten away lively people like yourself by your extreme faultlessness? As we are just now speaking the entire truth, I must confess that excessive conceit appears to be one of these small faults of yours, that you deem so charming.'

'Now, you are laughing at me,' said Flora, half vexed, and half amused; 'but do you not really think yourself that some people are *too* good.'

'*Too* good, Flora!' said Mrs. Leslie gravely; 'can any human being be good at all? Too good is no word to apply to even the best and wisest of mankind. Has any man ever approached nearly to the goodness of our divine model? No, my little erring friend you think too lightly of these things. Trust me, there is no fault so trivial that it may wisely be let alone, and not battled with, and no fault that is really in the least pleasing. Pray, believe this, and now let us follow Caroline.'

'*She* has kept fast to her object, you see,' said Flora; 'she did not even wait to hear our discussion.' And they followed her through the first room full of curiosities into a small inner apartment, where stood the aquarium. This was a large glass case, the four sides and the bottom being of glass, and the top open to the air.

It was filled with sea water; but these receptacles for marine curiosities are now so well known, that I need not particularly describe it. Flora and Caroline, however, had not before seen one of these glass cases or its inhabitants, therefore to them it was novel and interesting. Caroline was standing by the glass, with her attention fixed on some of its strange contents. 'Oh, mamma!' she exclaimed when they entered, 'how long you have stayed talking out there. Do come, Flora, look at this lovely little pink flower spreading out its leaves on the top of a curious lump of pinkish brown stuff. I know it is a live animal, but it is much more like a flower.'

'It is indeed very like a flower,' cried Flora; 'and look at its necklace of bright blue beads; now, Mrs Leslie, is it true that this is an animal? Do you believe that yourself?'

'It is truly a living creature,' said Mrs Leslie; 'it can eat, digest its food, and move from place to place by its own free will. It is one of a class of creatures called Anthozoa, or living flowers. There are an immense variety of species of this singular portion of creation, and this is an Actinia, one of the commonest. That is, it may be found on every coast. Now, look on this side of the glass, Flora, here are two or three closed up, and just as you will find them sticking on the rocks.'

'Just like small round lumps of brown jelly,' said Flora.

'This one has little green stripes all over it,' said Caroline; 'and, mamma, where do the leaves of the flower-like top come from? I do not see any signs of them on these closed ones.'

'The leaves, or tentacles, for they are in fact the creature's arms, or feelers, are now folded up and enclosed in the outer skin, which is drawn together at the top like a bag. The mouth is in the middle of these arms.'

'How I should like to see it eat!'

'It will eat insects or small mussels; it seizes its food with all its tentacles, and gradually pulls or tucks it into its mouth. It is curious what strength there is in these small, soft, and delicate-looking feelers.'

'Look, look, the green one is unwrapping!' cried Flora; 'how curious, it is even prettier than the pink one.'

'The full name of this little being,' said Mrs Leslie,

'is Actinia Mesembryanthemum. Now, observe, both of you, how it holds itself on to the glass.'

'Its skin is stretched out like a sucker,' said Caroline, 'and clings to the glass.'

'Yes; and in that way it fixes itself firmly to the rocks and must be detached very gently and carefully; for if you tear or wound the delicate base, you will kill the animal. You must take a silver knife or small paper-cutter, and pick it away by degrees.'

'But we have not a glass case like this; if we find any, where can we keep them?'

'I will show you how to place them on stones in an open basin, it does just as well.'

'Now, come here, Caroline,' cried Flora, 'what do you think is this green stuff crawling along? Why, it is a crab, and he has actually covered himself with bits of moss and green sea-weed, till he looks like anything but himself.'

'The common name of that curious fellow is the Vanity Crab,' said Mrs Leslie; 'he really does dress himself up in any loose bits of vegetation that he finds. Whether his purpose is warmth, or to hide himself from some marine enemy, or whether it is simply conceit, can be only matter of conjecture.'

'I am sure that it is conceit, mamma,' said Caroline; 'he is actually walking on his toes in the most fussy manner.'

'Here is a very large crab,' cried Flora; 'and here is a star fish!'

'Those star fish are most singular creatures,' said Mrs Leslie; 'we will catch one on the rocks, and you shall see its curious feet, and see it eat.'

'Here is a beautiful little fish,' continued Flora, who was darting round and round the glass case, stopping long at nothing; 'and here is a thing shaped like the actinia, but quite white!'

'That kind,' said Mrs Leslie, 'is brought by the fishermen from the deep sea; you see it is much larger than the green and pink ones; it is caught occasionally in the fishing nets, but it is not found on the rocks that are left bare at low tide. Indeed, all the more rare creatures of this species are found in deep sea, and can only be obtained by the dredging net.'

'Well, mamma, if we collect all that we can find ourselves first, perhaps you will ask some of the fishermen to bring us back a few of the better sorts?'

'Yes; I shall not object to that; and, now, shall we go down for a short time on the beach, as we proposed?'

'Oh! first, mamma,' exclaimed Caroline, 'do let us stay a little longer to look at this very wonderful actinia; it is something like the others, but so much more beautiful. Its feelers are thicker and shorter, and striped also.'

'And what a lovely colour,' cried Flora; 'it is salmon colour, is it not?"

'Yes; and it is a very handsome specimen,' said Mrs Leslie; 'these are more difficult to find than the first you looked at, because they bury themselves in the sand, or cover themselves with gravel and bits of stone; and often, when looking most carefully, you pass them by.'

'Are they always of the same colour, mamma?'

'No; their tints are most various, pale lilac, and pink, and delicate shades of green, and a pale brown; in short, almost every colour; I should like you to find one of these, because they assume so many different shapes, that it is most interesting to watch them. Sometimes they blow themselves out into a sort of thin bladder, which quite hides the tentacles, and is sometimes beautifully striped; but I have heard that it only does this when the base has been injured in taking it; and, altogether, it is more rare and much more delicate than the *mesembryanthemum.*'

'What is the name of this beautiful and rare one, mamma?' asked Caroline, as they left the museum.

'This one is *Buxodes Crassicornis.*'

'Do let us find some for ourselves, Caroline,' cried Flora, and they hurried down to the shore; but the tide was coming up, had just turned, so Mrs Leslie thought they were safer away from the slippery rocks, and promised to come down with them the next day at the time that the tide was going down, so that they might have at least a good hour's search on the rocks. They therefore took a walk along the dry sand, Caroline quite content with watching her favourite waves, and Flora looking forward to their success on the morrow.

'But, Caroline,' said she, as they parted, 'we shall have our morning walk as usual, eight o'clock, on the bridge.'

The next morning Flora was out the first, and she sprang to meet Caroline with a very important countenance. 'I have some news for you, Caroline,' said she; 'and you shall guess what it is as we go down the hill.'

'Is it something that gives you great pleasure?' asked Caroline, as they walked on arm in arm.

'Oh! yes, the very greatest pleasure; come, now, guess quickly.'

'I dare say your mamma has given you a nice glass aquarium to put your actinia in when you find them.'

'No! no! something far nicer than that.'

'Well, then, she has sent for your pony, that you may enjoy some rides on these smooth sands.'

'Oh! no, Caroline; cannot you think of something that would please me far more than such things as those?'

'I believe I shall not be able to guess it,' said Caroline. 'Please tell me, Flora.'

'It is about those pretty girls. Now guess.'

'It must be, then, that your mamma is acquainted with them, and will take you to see them.'

'Yes, that is just the thing; mamma knows their mamma; she is Lady Seymour, and I am to go with her to-morrow to call. So I shall know the three girls, and can introduce them to you!'

'I do not at all care about them,' said Caroline, 'but if they come to walk with us, I suppose I shall know them.'

'You *will* care about them, I am sure, for they must be such very nice girls.'

'Why do you feel so sure they are nice, Flora?'

'I do not know, but I do! Now do you remember that we argued before about that, and we will not argue again, but wait till we see.'

'Will you ask them to walk with us, then? I shall be quite afraid of speaking to them; I think they will not like me. Even you, Flora, think me dull and tiresome sometimes, though you have been my companion so long.'

'I dare say they will like me the best,' said Flora, 'because I am the liveliest, and talk the most to strangers. I wonder whether we shall see them this morning?'

'I hope not. I want to have you to myself as long

as I can. Let us go on the shore, and I will tell you how I am going to keep my actinias. Mamma will give me a large common red pottery basin or tub, and I shall put in it a collection of pretty stones, and bits of rock, with some sea-weed, and as soon as the sea-weed grows properly, I shall also put in some marine creatures.'

'Oh, Caroline, how silly you are! Do you think sea-weed and fishes will live in a dry red tub?'

'Not dry, of course, Flora! I meant to say that it is to be filled with sea water, and the sea-weed is to purify the water, and keep it fit for the creatures.'

'But it will be very ugly, Caroline. Where do you mean to keep it?'

'In the drawing-room on a low stool.'

'I think I shall not like to have any of these things, unless mamma will give me a real nice aquarium for them.'

'But it is thought that they will live quite as well, if not better, in a flat open tub, without so much water. So I am quite eager to try it. We will go upon the rocks this afternoon—shall we not, Flora?—and begin collecting them.'

'Yes, I can come to-day, but to-morrow I shall be out with mamma.'

'And I shall have to walk alone with my mamma; it will seem quite strange to be without you, Flora.'

'It will only be for one day, for the day after to-morrow most likely we shall all walk together. Now we must go back. How are you getting on with your lessons now?'

'Quite well; but I did not the first day or two, because the different room, and the different hours, put me out—I liked my old way best.'

'I never saw such a girl for old things as you are, Caroline.'

'But just now,' replied Caroline, 'I am eager to fill my new red tub, so do not be late this afternoon.'

And it was before the usual hour when they met again in the square.

CHAPTER IV.

Come along, Flora,' cried Caroline, 'let us make the most of this day, as we shall not have a walk together to-morrow. See, I have a basket with a tin put inside it for carrying home the stones and sea-weed, to prepare my house for the actinia.'

'Well, I must help you, I suppose?' replied Flora, 'as I am not ready myself to collect any; I have neither glass case nor red pan for them yet.'

'Mamma has given me a beautiful large crockery tub.'

'I cannot say much for its good looks, Caroline,'

said Mrs Leslie; '*you* must make its beauty by filling it with lovely and curious objects. Now we must go down quite upon the rocks, or we shall find neither sea-weeds nor actinia; the tide is very suitable this afternoon, as it has left some rocks uncovered for us to commence with, and we can follow it as it recedes.'

'Why, mamma, the rocks are quite grown over with this slippery brown sea-weed, we shall never get along upon it.'

'Oh! what disagreeable wet stuff,' cried Flora, as she slid about, with difficulty keeping on her feet. 'Do you like this, Mrs Leslie?'

'I do not at all mind it,' she replied; 'this is the common wrack, which is abundant on most shores. You must not go so fast, Flora! Walk gently, and plant your feet firmly at each step, and then you will find it easy enough to walk.'

'Where shall we find the pretty sea-weeds and some actinia, mamma? Are they amongst this brown wrack?'

'We shall find them in the little pools between the rocks—here is one! a sort of break, you see, in the rocks, full of sea water. Do you see, Caroline, that there are varieties of small and pretty sea-weeds growing on the sides of the pool. We shall take some of those and endeavour to make them grow as nicely in your earthenware pan.'

'Here,' said Flora, 'is a pretty feathery-looking

pink one! Shall I pull it up? I will turn back my sleeve!' So saying, she knelt on the side of the pool, and stretched out her bare arm to reach the weed, but it was deeper in the water than she imagined, and losing her balance on the slippery edge, she would have had a complete bath in the pool had not Mrs Leslie watched her, and caught her firmly by the arm.

'Oh! how nearly I was in the water, Mrs Leslie! What a dip I should have had. How can we reach the weeds, they are in such deep water?'

'You must not pull them up without their roots, otherwise they will soon die,' said Mrs Leslie. 'We will try to break off a little piece of the rock on which they grow. You have a long and sharp chisel in your basket, Caroline; give it to me, and we will try to take up that little green sea-weed which is much nearer the top.'

'Do you mean this broad-leaved one, mamma? It is not nearly so pretty as the pink bit Flora was trying to reach.'

'No! it is not so pretty, but it is the best suited for your purpose. This green laver will keep the sea water fresh and good, far better than any other of the sea-weeds, so we will take two or three little plants of it.' And stooping carefully, Mrs. Leslie struck off with her chisel a large piece of rock, with the delicate little plant attached to it.

'That is famous!' cried Flora; 'surely that will grow very well?'

'Yes, I dare say it will,' replied Mrs Leslie. 'Now look about for any other green sorts, they are the best.'

'I do believe, mamma,' exclaimed Caroline, 'that I see one of the little pink actinia rather low down in the water; come round and look.'

'Yes, indeed, I see three or four, but only one is spread out. You see we shall have no difficulty in finding inhabitants for your aquarium. In the very first pool we examine here are several.'

'May I not take one to-day, mamma?'

'I advise you not to do so, for their home in the drawing-room will not be fit for their reception to-day. Have patience until you have some plants of sea-weed growing nicely, and the water looking clear and fresh; to take these little creatures otherwise would be wanton cruelty.'

'Come then, Flora, let us go to another pool and find sea-weeds. Mamma, will you take charge of my tin with the green laver in it?'

'Certainly! give me your basket and go further on; try to find the sea-grass, it has a long, flat green leaf, and is most probably plentiful here; indeed you may take any green ones that you can find.'

So they went on, peeping into all the little pools, and searching along the edges of the rocks. They soon learnt to keep their footing on the slippery wrack.

'Oh! how pleasant this is, mamma,' said Caroline; 'such a lovely bright day, and finding these weeds is so amusing, and then I have Flora all to myself to-day!'

'Are you not to have her any more to yourself, do you mean, Caroline?'

'Not quite, mamma! for she is to know some other little girls who are staying here.'

'Well, that will perhaps be pleasure for both of you; it is as well sometimes to see others besides our own constant friends.'

Flora clapped her hands! 'There, Caroline, I am so glad your mamma thinks so. Do you know, Mrs Leslie, that Caroline has been really vexed at the idea of my having other companions besides herself; but you do not see any harm in it, do you?'

'No, indeed, Flora; and I cannot believe that Caroline would be so selfish as to deny you the pleasure of some pleasant acquaintances.'

'Oh no, mamma, I do not wish to do so; I only said that I never wished for any one but Flora, and I felt as if she cared less for me, because she was so very eager to know these other little girls.'

'You must learn, dear Caroline, to be less exclusive in your friendships. But what have you there?'

'A nice little green weed, mamma, but I am afraid

I have taken no rock with it, but have pulled it quite off. Will it grow, do you think?'

'You have the root tolerably entire, so we will try. It is a pretty little thing, and is called Bryopsis; this one will do very well for you, and I think if we take one other species, it will be sufficient for your small aquarium.'

'Here it is then,' cried Flora; 'is not this the sea-grass you spoke of? Pray let me try to knock it off with its bit of rock. I will not be awkward this time.' So she took the chisel and succeeded in obtaining the plant quite whole, root and all.

'There is a little crab,' cried she; 'will you keep crabs also, Caroline?'

'I think I should like to have two or three very tiny, pretty little crabs: can I, mamma?'

'Yes, certainly, they will live wherever the actinia can live; but, as I said before, settle their abode nicely first.

'Now, mamma, you say we have plenty of sea-weed, but would it do any harm to put in one of the pretty feathery pink ones?'

'You can try one, it is named Plocamium. I do not know whether it will do well, but take it, and we shall see. And a piece of coralline would look very pretty; see! here is a fine bunch; let me knock off this piece for you, and then I think you need only collect a few pebbles and bits of rock, and we are provided for to-day.'

'But, mamma, I shall want a great deal more sea water than I can take in this little tin.'

'Indeed, you will; I shall send down to the shore for a good bucketful for you, or two, if required.'

'And then, mamma, shall I be ready to fetch some live creatures to-morrow?'

'I would let the sea-weeds settle for a day or two, and not put in anything living during to-morrow and the following day; and I am sure you will not be so impatient as to spoil the aquarium through foolish hurry.'

'No, I will not. Oh, mamma, are you turning homewards already?'

'It is quite late enough for us to turn; you see it takes a long time to go across these slippery rocks; and, besides, the tide will turn soon, and then we should indeed have to hurry.'

'I had quite forgotten the tide,' said Flora; 'it would soon catch us, I suppose? Come, Caroline, let us go quickly.'

More than one tumble occurred during the walk, or rather scramble, back to the dry sands; but luckily Mrs Leslie had charge of the precious tin, so no damage was done, excepting a little wetting of frocks and shoes.

'We shall walk in the morning together, shall we not, Flora, as you will not go to call on the little girls till the afternoon?'

'Of course, we shall walk every morning as usual,' replied Flora; 'so, good-night.'

Caroline was extremely busy that evening in arranging her earthenware pan, the pebbles and bits of rock were nicely disposed at the bottom, and the plants of sea-weed placed carefully round the edges. Then the sea water, for which her mamma sent, was gently poured in, and the sea-weeds expanded their leaves as if they were quite happy to be again in their native element.

'I hope they will be as nice and fresh to-morrow, mamma,' said Caroline, as she went to bed. 'I shall look at them the very first thing.'

'It is all right, Flora,' cried Caroline, when they met the next morning on the bridge.

'What is all right?' asked she.

'Why, the sea water and the weeds; the sea-grass is all spread out so nicely, and the beautiful small Bryopsis looks quite like tiny feathers, and the laver very fresh, and the sea water is clear and nice; I am so glad it is going to answer well.'

'So am I; when I see how yours goes on I shall try to make an aquarium for myself.'

'I am rather surprised, Flora, that you have not already begun, for you are generally so very much delighted with anything that is new; but this time *I* am the one to be most eager about this new amusement.'

'I should have been so too, Caroline, but that just now I am more interested about the new friends I am to have. That is what has put me off from thinking about aquariums and pebbles, and all such things; but I dare say I shall have as good an one as you before we leave the sea shore.'

'Do you mean when you have become tired of your new friends?' asked Caroline, rather maliciously.

'Now, that is too bad, Caroline, I do not mean to tire of them or of you either. So make up your mind to take a walk with me and with them to-morrow, for I shall ask them to accompany us, and no doubt they will consent. We will go up to the castle, if your mamma will take us.'

'She said she would do so some day, so I will ask her to let it be to-morrow; and to-day I think I shall ask her to go with me round that point, as far as Carnelian Bay.'

'But *I* should like to go there; will you leave it to-day, and go some day when I am with you.'

'I only mentioned it because I do not know where to go to-day; you know my sea water is to be left to settle, so I cannot collect actinia to-day. I might go to the museum, but you would like that too; so I do not know which to choose.'

'I will choose for you; go to the museum to-day, and we will walk to Carnelian Bay all together.'

'Very well, Flora, I shall do so; **and now, I**

suppose, I must say good-bye till to-morrow morning?'

'Yes; I shall have so much to tell you about Lady Seymour's daughters.'

'And I shall tell you about the museum; good-bye.'

Mrs Leslie willingly went with Caroline to the museum, where she was soon quite engrossed with the variety of curiosities of all sorts. In the first room, what interested her most was the skeleton of an ancient Briton, which had been found in a coffin hollowed from the trunk of an oak tree. This skeleton was very perfect, and fixed together with wires; the teeth even being quite entire. The bones were perfectly black, either from their very great age, or from the staining quality of the oak wood.

'Mamma, is it possible,' said Caroline, 'that these black bones were once part of a grand old ancient Briton; perhaps a Druid?'

'It is supposed that this is the skeleton of a warrior, or perhaps some sort of chief or king, from the care with which he was buried, and the remains of weapons and ornaments which were enclosed in the coffin; but I do not see any very strong reason why it should not have been a Druid.'

'Oh, mamma; and once walked about in a long white dress, making horrible sacrifices, and worshipping mistletoes!'

'It is indeed difficult to realise, especially when you

consider the immense age of these bones. Can you, Caroline, tell me about how long since this Druid or ancient Briton was a living man upon the earth?'

'I cannot say at once, mamma; but I think I could nearly make out, by considering about it. Flora would tell you the date directly.'

'Well, if you cannot directly, consider about it, and let me hear you consider aloud, that I may understand how you arrive at your conclusion.'

'Well, mamma, the Druids were found with the other Britons in England by Julius Cæsar (oh! how often I have wondered how they first got there); and the Romans came to England 54 years before Christ. Now, it is 1862 years after the birth of Christ; so, supposing this great black skeleton to have been alive when Julius Cæsar came, it must have been 54 years added to 1862—that is, 1916 years old. Is that about right, mamma?'

'Yes, probably that may be about its age. Do you not find it pleasant, Caroline, to be able to decide about the probable age of different things?'

'Oh, very pleasant, mamma; and did the Britons always bury in oak tree trunks?'

'I cannot say that, for certain, there is so very little actually known about them. You can see in this glass case some bits of the ornaments and weapons that were buried with the skeleton; and it is these things chiefly that decide the question as to whether this *was* an ancient Briton! For, after the Roman invasion, arms, and tools, and ornaments quite changed their character.'

'Now, mamma, shall we look at something else?'

'Yes; we will go up stairs.'

On the stairs were arranged some javelins and spears, from different savage tribes, and the sharp jagged spike of a sword fish; all of which attracted Caroline's attention. The upper room was very pretty; round it were ranged stuffed animals and birds of every species in glass cases; and the tables in the middle contained excellent specimens of minerals, polished pebbles, marbles, madrepores, corals, and so on.

'I scarcely know where to begin, mamma,' said Caroline; 'such a number of delightful and beautiful things. I will look at the birds first, for I see many that I do not in the least recognise.'

'Well, dear Caroline, mount up on those steps, which you will see are made purposely to go round the room, and to look into the upper glasses.'

Caroline went up to the little stand at the top, and found that there was a handle to move the wheels on which the ladder was fixed, so that she could move herself all along the glass cases without descending.

The golden pheasant she thought she admired the most of all the birds; and a very handsome brown bustard. Her mother sat down whilst Caroline's circuit was made, and answered all the questions that were showered upon her; Caroline was so well amused that she scarcely had time to lament the absence of Flora.

After the birds, they went up to the gallery that runs round the top of the room; and here were cases that much delighted Caroline; beautiful specimens of carnelians, and all sea-shore pebbles; her mamma was able to show her all the varieties of which they had been talking, and some of these had been found on the Yorkshire coast; but the handsomer specimens were all from southern shores.

'Oh, mamma, I am afraid we shall never pick up any very good stones here; you see how much prettier these Bognor moss agates are, and many others.'

'Still, Caroline, I think you may find very nice carnelians, and fortification agates on this shore; at any rate you must be content with such as there are. We will go to Carnelian Bay to-morrow, if you like.'

'Yes, mamma; I dare say Flora can come to-morrow, and I would rather not go without her.'

'You must not be too much disappointed, Caroline, if Flora should spend a great part of her time with these little Seymours whilst we are here. You know that she is fond of novelty, and she feels that she can enjoy your society every day whilst we are at home. Therefore, let her think much of these chance acquaintances, without allowing yourself to be disturbed by her doing so; you must remember, my dear child, that you cannot hope always to keep her to yourself.'

'I do not wish to do so, mamma, and I am glad she should have some novelty and pleasure; but I do not believe that she can quite desert me, even for the short time we shall be here. *I* could not leave her to go to strangers.'

'You must not judge Flora by yourself; she is of so different a nature. Make allowances, dear Caroline, for her lively excitable disposition, and be satisfied with the portion of love you have from her, which I truly believe is very great. Do you not think that she really loves you?'

'Indeed, I do, mamma; that is what makes me say that she cannot leave me for the company of strangers.'

'We will hope that she will not; and now we will leave the museum; perhaps Flora will come also the next time we visit it, and there are numbers of beautiful objects that we have not yet examined.'

'Indeed there are; I am sure I could stay here all day without tiring at all.'

'A little at a time is better than too much of this sort of thing; let us now breathe the fresh sea air before we go in.'

'On Monday I might bring home some actinia for the aquarium; and if we go to Carnelian Bay, I can collect them as we return home.'

'Yes; that will be a good plan.'

'Well, Flora, how did you like the little girls?' asked Caroline, when they met the next week.

'Oh! so much; they are most delightful; they were all in the drawing-room when we went in, and the eldest came and talked to me a little bit; and then Lady Seymour said they had better go out as usual, and asked me to go with them; so I left mamma there, and came into the Spa garden with them; we sat and talked in the arbours, and ran about the walks.'

'How old are they?'

'The eldest, Augusta, is a year older than I am; and the second, Alice, is the same age.'

'And what did they talk about?'

'Indeed, they talked a great deal; they told me what they learnt, and how they went on at home. They have a governess living with them to teach them; but just now she is gone home for a holiday.'

'So they have their holiday, too, I suppose. Do they have lessons with their mamma at all?'

'No; I fancy not; I think they do nothing whilst they are here; but they are to make up for that when they go to London, which they do every year. Then they have music masters, and learn to dance at a large dancing academy. Oh! how I should like to go to London.'

'I would much rather be taught by my own mamma.'

'So would I, in preference to having a governess; but I should like the music masters and drawing masters.'

'I do not believe any music master could teach you better than your own mamma; what a beautiful pianist she is herself.'

'I dare say she is quite as good as any master; but still, I should like the fun of having the masters.'

'Well, what else did they talk about?'

'Oh! a great deal about their clothes; and I cannot say that is a subject which very much interests me; but they say that is because I have lived so much in the country, seeing few people, and those few perhaps not fashionably dressed; and that if I were in London every year as they are, I should take the same pleasure in having a new set of frocks, and collars, and capes, every season, made in the proper manner; and I dare say I should.'

'I do not believe you would ever become so frivolous, Flora, as to spend thought and time upon fashionable dressing.'

'I do not know why you should pronounce it frivolous,' replied Flora; 'most ladies do pay great attention to such things.'

'Our mammas do not, Flora; I never heard them talk about dresses and fashions, and yet they always look nice, and not different from other people.'

'They do not talk about it, certainly, but you know we do sometimes drive to H— purposely to buy materials for clothes of all sorts; and then mamma's maid has all sorts of pictures sent her every month with the shapes of things, so she knows how to make them. Then, you see, it is very easy to have the right sort of clothes without spending any time upon it; and one day's buying in every two or three months is enough to do it all.'

'That certainly suffices for our mammas; and I have always been glad when the day's shopping at H— was finished, because I thought it tiresome and stupid. But these Miss Seymours tell me that they go to shops regularly every afternoon, after the masters have gone; and they go and look at things in four or five different shops before they decide on buying anything; and really they seem to consider it a matter of great importance.'

'Well, then, I shall always call them frivolous. Where is there home in the country?'

'It is a good way from here, they did not talk much about that, except about some neighbours they have. London seems to be what they like best.'

'Then to-day, Flora, you will come and walk with me and mamma as usual; we have settled to go to

Carnelian Bay, and for me to collect some actinia on our way home, for my aquarium is now quite ready for them. You will be ready, will you not?'

Flora hesitated: 'I am not quite sure that I can go to-day, Caroline. Cannot you put off Carnelian Bay one day more. Augusta said they were going to drive to-day, and her mamma had allowed her to ask me to go with them, she ran up and asked when we went back to their door; and as it is the first time they have invited me, it would be rude to refuse.'

Caroline looked annoyed. 'Then I shall not see you again to-day, Flora?'

'No,' she replied laughing. 'Cannot you live without me one other afternoon? To-morrow I will walk with you.'

'You never asked me what I saw at the museum yesterday, or what I did, but I will tell you about that another time.' And Caroline went home with a more lingering step than was usual with her. Her papa and mamma were at breakfast when she entered.

'Oh, mamma, I am sorry I am so late,' she said; 'it is the first time, is it not? I came from the bridge quite slowly.'

'That is not your general method of progressing, Caroline,' said her father, putting his arm round her; 'nor is this so joyous a face as you have brought us from the shore during the last week. What is the matter? Did you find the green laver drooping this morning, or the sea water in the red tub muddy?'

'Oh no, papa, I should not look sorry for such little things as that, but I *am* sorry for something.'

'I can guess what it is,' said her mother; 'Flora is again engaged for the afternoon with her new friends.'

'Yes, mamma, indeed she is; so I am left again, and I do not like it.'

'Is this actually,' said her father, 'the second afternoon that Flora has not spent some hours with you! That is certainly dreadful, especially as you have only your mamma left to speak to!'

'Oh, papa!' exclaimed Caroline, 'you wish to laugh at me, and I dare say it seems foolish to a man; and you think I do not value having mamma to walk with me, but I really do; and I will try not to be put out of my happiness by missing Flora.'

'You will do wisely, dear little girl,' her father replied, 'not to let such small vexations affect your spirits.'

'Caroline has not yet arrived at thinking Flora's absence a *small* vexation,' said her mother, smiling. 'But we shall try to spend a pleasant afternoon, Caroline; is it to be Carnelian Bay to-day?'

'No, mamma, I should like to wait one more day for Flora. What can we do to-day?'

'Suppose we take quite a country walk, to Oliver's Mount.'

No sea shore, mamma! No actinia?'

'We were to leave them for the return from Carnelian Bay, and perhaps it is as well not to be too much engrossed with sea-shore beauties all at once; you might tire of them.'

'Well, mamma, I will leave my sea water and sea-weeds to themselves one more day, and to-morrow I will determine to go and have a real hunt for live creatures to enjoy my tub!'

'And now for our lessons, Caroline.'

CHAPTER V.

A FINE afternoon tempted them out earlier than usual, and they took the road leading up the hill from the Spa bridge.

'This road is very pleasant, mamma,' said Caroline, 'the shade of the trees is so nice; that is one thing that I do not like on the shore, the sun is so glaring, and of course there is no shade. So, often in the mornings Flora and I keep in the garden beneath the trees.'

'Sometimes the sunshine and sometimes the shade is pleasant, Caroline; a little variety in all things is, I think, better than always the same thing.'

'Excepting about friends and relations, mamma,

I never wish to have a variety of friends, and, of course, no one would like to change their own relations.'

'Surely not, the natural love that we have towards those of our own family can never be transferred, and is so wonderfully and strongly implanted, that ingratitude and unworthiness of all kinds does not generally destroy it, especially from fathers and mothers to their own children.'

'That reminds me of something, mamma; do you know what I mean?'

'I think I do, but tell me in your own words.'

'I cannot very well express it, mamma, but that fathers and mothers always continue to love their own children, seems a little in the same sort of way that God always loves men although they are bad. And perhaps that is a small relic of the likeness to God in which we were made. Do you understand, mamma?'

'Yes, dear child, I think you have expressed your idea very fairly, and I quite agree with you that the much enduring love between relations is one of the least faulty of all human feelings, for it is entirely unselfish.'

'Then you do not think love of friends is quite so good, mamma, because there is something selfish in that? You know Flora said I was selfish to wish to keep her quite to myself.'

'She was partly right; very exclusive friendship *is* selfish. You know that I mean friendship that is desirous of excluding all others from the love of your friend.'

'I shall try not to feel that, mamma. Then you think it is a good plan to know many people, and to love more than one?'

'Perhaps we always have one friend that suits us better, and that we love better than any other, and I do not object to that. What I wish you to perceive, Caroline, is, that Flora may know and love several others, and that you also may enjoy the society of other girls without in the least diminishing your friendship for each other. On the contrary, you will return to your pleasant home intercourse with her with the greater pleasure, from having found that others, who are affectionate and pleasing, do not, after all, suit you so well. As you grow up you will leave home oftener, and what has occurred here may then often happen, so learn to use the circumstance in its right way, not to turn it into a difficulty and a sorrow.'

'I will not, mamma. Was there not one great friendship mentioned in the Bible?'

'Yes; between David and Jonathan. Do you remember much about it?'

'No, mamma; I should like to read it again.'

'Do so; and tell me what you think of it during

our next lonely walk, that is to say, our next walk without Flora.'

'Yes, mamma. Now we have left the trees, this road has become very ugly, and it is dusty; I do not like this so well as the sea shore.'

'We shall turn presently and go up the steep side of the mount, on the grass; then we will rest for a time under the trees, as you are so fond of shade, and then we will go on the top of the hill and look over the wide sea.'

'There is a large new house building,' said Caroline, as they turned. 'What an uncomfortable looking thing a new house is—so bare—and all the piles of mortar and bricks lying about.'

'That building is to be a large hotel, showing that Scarborough is an increasing place. I agree with you that a new house is not a pretty object.'

'No, mamma; new buildings are ugly, and generally old ones are pretty and picturesque, ruins I mean.'

'Yes, it is strange, for the one tells of decay and death, and of the short-lived uncertainty of all human doings and undertakings; and the other shows prosperity and hope. This great hotel, for instance, shows that this particular town is growing in importance, and that its visitors are yearly on the increase. That will bring work and money to its poorer inhabitants, who, I doubt not, look with pleasure on every new abode that springs up.'

'Do other towns increase in size as this has done, mamma? You know you said that a few years since there was only the old fishing town here. Have all the people come here from other places?'

'Almost every town in England is growing rapidly; there is no need for people to come from other places, for every year the number increases in all towns and villages.'

'So the world becomes fuller and fuller. In time, mamma, there will scarcely be room for all the people.'

'This little island of ours is certainly becoming very full, I believe more so for its size than any country in the world, excepting China; but it will be very long before all parts of the world are full of inhabitants in the same way. Think of your maps, and try to tell me of some places that have scarcely any inhabitants.'

'Oh! do you mean the Great Desert in Africa, that has no inhabitants? But I thought people could not live there, because there is nothing but sand, and no plants will grow.'

'Indeed I think the world will be in a very crowded state before people will resort to the desert for an abode. But there are many other places in the world which are beautiful and pleasant to live in, and which hitherto have been scarcely ever seen by human beings. Now let us mount this steep field, and we will rest at the top, beneath those trees, and then we can talk more.'

Caroline had indeed no breath left for talking before she had gone far up the hill; it was almost a climb, so abrupt is the rise of Oliver's Mount on the north side. Panting and heated, she flung herself down on the grass beside her mother, as soon as they arrived under the shade of the little wood that crowns the ascent.

'That was a good climb, mamma,' she said; 'and how pleasant it is to rest here and look over this wide view; how pretty the castle-hill looks, and the pier and harbour.'

'Yes; and the lovely blue sea, with ships dotted about here and there.'

'Why is this hill called Oliver's Mount, mamma?' asked Caroline.

'I have not been able to discover when, precisely, that name was given; but doubtless it was in consequence of Cromwell's having used this hill as a good situation for a camp, or for some such warlike purpose in the course of the civil war with Charles, during which the castle was destroyed.'

'Well, mamma, I wish it had another name; anything to do with Cromwell never pleases me.'

'He was very clever, and came in well for the times, which required some such bold spirit to overthrow much that was bad; but I agree with you, that he was not a pleasant personage.'

'Now, that we can look over so wide a space, it seems to me that just about here the world is not so very full as you were saying at the bottom of the hill. Look at all those fields with not a single house upon them, and those low hills, and all along that shore. Why, mamma, there is room for hundreds and thousands more houses.'

'Yes, certainly there is, if you wish the whole country to be like a town, closely packed with houses, only having streets and lanes for people to pass along; but were it so, Caroline, where would you have corn grow; where would you send cattle to pasture; where would your hayfields be—in short whence would come necessary supplies of all kinds?'

'Oh, mamma, I never thought of all those things; how very stupid it was; of course, the people in every town must have a certain quantity of land for their food to grow upon in different ways.'

'Is the supply of our food the only thing for which space is wanted?'

'Yes; I think so, mamma; I include in that, grass for cows in order to give us milk and butter and cheese; and pasture for the creatures we eat; and garden ground for potatoes and vegetables; and wheat fields for bread, and barley fields for beer; that is all, mamma.'

'Where is our wood to come from for house-building and furniture, and an endless variety of common purposes for which we want wood? Where are our bricks or stones to come from?'

'Stop, mamma; I quite forgot that we must have woods and plantations of all sorts, and brick fields and stone quarries; indeed, each houseful of people must use a large space of earth besides the house they live in, if we consider all our wants in so many different ways. I cannot think how it is managed in such a place as London; I wonder there is not a famine and a scarcity made in the country round.'

'It would soon indeed be the case, were all in London to be kept by the produce of the adjacent country; but you surely know that things of all sorts are perpetually passing up to London from every quarter, not only of our own land, but from all parts of the world — corn, meat, fish, and so on. Those places where there are not enough persons to consume the produce of the country, send their overplus to such towns as London.'

'Then the best way would be, mamma, for a great many of the people from the crowded places to go away to other countries, where there is more than enough for the inhabitants.'

'What would you call such a proceeding, Caroline? It is a very common event; and you must frequently have heard it mentioned as—Emigration.'

'Oh, mamma, how silly I am. Of course I have heard of that, often; and I know it means that people leave their own country to settle and live elsewhere; but I never thought about the reason; it is that they find more room and more abundance in other lands.'

'Yes; can you tell me to what countries the English have chiefly emigrated?'

'I think, to Australia.'

'That is one land that has swallowed up a very large number of our countrymen; but there is another large country, pretty thickly inhabited by a people who are almost all from Great Britain or Ireland.'

'I know; it is Canada.'

'And beyond Canada, think of the large territory that stretches away to the Pacific, scarcely yet even sprinkled with settlers; there is, indeed, no fear of England becoming quite overwhelmed with its own inhabitants, whilst we have so glorious a land to which we can resort. Emigration is a most interesting subject.'

'Do not you think, mamma, that it must be very dreadful to leave one's home and country for ever, intending to live for all the rest of one's life in Australia or America?'

'Generally whole families emigrate together; then, you know, there is no one left behind to regret.'

'No one of quite one's own family; but there might be some very dear friend, and many acquaintances that we loved a little. Oh! I could not bear to emigrate, mamma, even if all the people I know went too. I should not like to go away from my old home for ever, never to see it again.'

'You are, you know, rather strongly attached to accustomed places, as well as familiar faces; and I also, Caroline, love my own home and country; I think I should very much dislike to emigrate; but we are happily and comfortably situated, we have a beautiful home, with abundance of everything; and persons so placed have, I think, no excuse for deserting their own land. But for those who are painfully struggling to live in England, the advantages offered by new countries should not be disregarded. Come, Caroline, let us resume our walk; at the top of this wood we shall come on an open space from which there is even a wider prospect than this.'

The walk through the wood was shady and refreshing; Caroline sought about for ferns and any plants that might be new to her; and her mother was glad to see that she could enjoy her walk tolerably without her usual companion.

'I am sorry to leave the wood, mamma,' she said, as they emerged on the barren top of the hill; 'but that yellow furze is very pretty.'

'Yes; there is always something pretty to be found

even in the most unpromising-looking places, and the view here is splendid.'

'I should like to live at the top of a hill, mamma.'

'For the sake of a wide extensive view it would be very nice; but I think I should prefer my home in a more sheltered place, and one more readily reached; I should be sorry to mount that steep hill every day, and perhaps twice in a day.'

'I dare say, after all, our own home is better placed, on level ground among the trees—our own pretty home—I shall be very glad to return, mamma; but I am afraid Flora will not, she will regret those pretty lively girls, and be perhaps very tired of me.'

'Do not anticipate such vexations, dear Caroline,' replied her mother; 'perhaps Flora will be more happy to return to your society than you would fancy. Now, we shall walk along this road, which will lead us round the crown of the hill, and then we shall descend by the carriage road on the other side; we shall have a nice view of the shore all along this side.'

Caroline gathered a large bunch of the bright yellow furze flowers; and the air that blew from the sea was so fresh and exhilarating, that she almost forgot her trouble about Flora in the enjoyment of the bright day, and in listening to the singing of many larks above her head, but out of sight. When they had gone round the top of the hill, a distance of about half a mile, they found themselves on the western, or land side, and now looked only upon a valley, and some low hills beyond. Soon they began to descend by a carriage road, and a little way down, the hill side was thickly clothed with trees, under the shade of which they passed pleasantly, until they again reached the new hotel, and the stile over which they had climbed in order to mount the hill.

'I declare, mamma,' exclaimed Caroline, 'we have gone quite round Oliver's Mount; what a pleasant walk we have had; and it is down hill now all the way into the town, so you will not be tired. You are very kind, mamma, to walk about with me so much, —much more than you do at home.'

'When we are at home, dear Caroline, you are in our own grounds; and even if you go out to the village, it is all amongst people who know you well. I could not let you run about alone in a place like this; nor do I think you would like it; I do allow you and Flora to be together on the shore, or in the garden in the early morning; but I should not wish you to go into the town with no one but her.'

'No, mamma, I should not like it myself; and I am glad to be with you more; I can talk to you more than I did at home.'

'You see, Caroline,' said her mother, smiling, 'there is even some advantage in Flora's absence, and in being away from home; you have more of my company, and, as you say, talk a great deal more.

Now, if Flora were here, you would probably be running about, before me or behind me, and not conversing at all.'

'That is quite true; and though Flora talks always a great deal, she cannot of course tell me so much as you do; and she often says things that I do not agree with, and then we argue a little.'

'That is very well; arguing will oblige you to bring forward all your own reasons for thinking one way or another way, and will lead you to forming some opinions of your own about everything that is passing; but you must remember that the object of argument is to convince, and so do not forget that your own opinions may be wrongly formed; and if you feel convinced by Flora, always acknowledge it at once.'

'Yes, mamma, I hope I shall; and I hope she will give me an opportunity to-morrow, by coming to walk with us, and arguing, all the way.'

But the next morning brought no such pleasure to Caroline; she had never anticipated that her early walk with Flora before breakfast would be broken in upon. It seemed to her quite sufficiently vexatious, that day after day should pass and see Flora's whole afternoon devoted to her new friends; so she ran joyously down to the bridge at the usual time, intending to give Flora a minute account of Oliver's Mount; and she took her usual place on the middle of the bridge, and looked down on the people moving about far below, for some time very contentedly. At last she began to think, 'Flora is very late, I will go up towards her house to meet her;' but she arrived at the door without seeing anything of Flora. She stood undecided for a time, and then thought she would ring and ask; perhaps Flora was not well; the thought quickened her hand, and the pull she gave to the bell soon brought some one to the door.

'Is Miss Staunton not well this morning?' asked Caroline, breathlessly.

'She is quite well, miss,' replied the man; 'she went out as usual about half-an-hour since.'

Caroline turned away without speaking. Where then could Flora be? It was very odd that she had not waited on the bridge for her; perhaps she was a little further on in the garden. She ran back, across the bridge, and down the walk, but could see nothing of Flora. Surely she cannot have gone to walk with those Miss Seymours without even telling me, or asking me to come, thought Caroline, as she slowly descended the steps leading to the terrace and concert rooms. There were but few persons on the terrace, and not seeing her friend among them, she leant upon the wall, and fixed her eyes on the waves that were gently splashing at its base. It was a lovely still morning, and Caroline fell into a reverie about the ever-moving wondrous ocean; about the countless precious treasures that are lying below the waves,

CAROLINE THINKING OF FLORA'S BEHAVIOUR.—*Page* 94.

never again to be looked upon by mortal eyes; about the many human beings above whose bodies that mysterious element has closed; about the living creatures, some terrible, some beautiful, some infinitely minute, some of gigantic dimensions; and her thoughts were very pleasantly running on to the endless variety of subjects connected with the blue waves beneath her feet, when she was roused by a light touch on her shoulder, and by Flora's voice.

'Why, Caroline,' she exclaimed, 'how immoveably you have been staring at the sea for the last ten minutes; we have been watching you, and wondering when you would stir!'

'We!' repeated Caroline, looking round, and at a little distance she saw Lady Seymour's three daughters, with amusement depicted in their faces; on meeting Caroline's glance, they turned away and slowly walked on. 'Oh, Flora!' said Caroline reproachfully, 'you might have come to tell me that you would not walk with me this morning; I have been waiting and looking for you everywhere; and I did not think that you would leave me in the morning as well as the afternoon.'

'I will not *every* morning,' replied Flora; 'but see, they are beckoning to me; I must run after them, so good-bye for the present.'

'Stay, Flora,' said Caroline, catching her dress;

G

'you are going with us this afternoon to Carnelian Bay, are you not? You know I put it off yesterday on purpose to wait for you.'

Flora hesitated. 'I don't quite know yet; they spoke of a ride on ponies this afternoon.'

'But if you have not yet agreed to go with them, you are not tied; and you *did* promise me to go to Carnelian Bay, so I consider you engaged to mamma and to me.'

'What time do you mean to start, Caroline?' asked Flora, eagerly looking after the three girls, who had nearly reached the end of the terrace.

'Why! the time that we always go out in the afternoon, you surely have not forgotten that.'

'Well, Caroline, if I am not with you when you are ready to start, you may suppose that I am gone to ride with Augusta and Harriet, and if they don't ride I will come with you. Now I must go.' And she ran quickly to overtake her friends, who appeared to laugh immoderately as Flora joined them.

'She might at least have asked me to walk with them,' thought Caroline, and her eyes filled with tears as she turned to go home. When she reached the top of the hill she sat down on a bench, and meditated on Flora's behaviour rather resentfully. This mood was not softened by Flora's touch again on her shoulder, and the words, 'It is settled, Caroline, that we are to ride to-day, so don't wait for me any longer, but go to Carnelian Bay when you like; I daresay I shall be very uncertain as long as the Seymours are here; good-bye!'

Caroline scarcely looked round, but she saw their figures retreating up one of the walks that led to the upper part of the garden, and she fancied she saw a mocking sort of smile on the lips of Augusta. With her heart full, she went home. 'Papa will laugh at me still more this morning,' she thought, as she opened the dining-room door. But her papa saw at a glance that she was in no humour for laughing, and simply giving her his morning kiss, he went on talking to Mrs Leslie.

'Well, Caroline,' said her mother, when Caroline had hastily swallowed her cup of tea, 'I see you have been vexed this morning, are we not to hear what has happened? I suppose Flora is again engaged for the afternoon with her new friends.'

'Worse than that, mamma,' said Caroline, trying not to cry; 'I waited a long time on the bridge for her, and then I went to the house to ask if she were ill, and heard that she had gone out long before. Then I looked about the garden for her, and at last I saw her walking with the three Miss Seymours, and she only spoke to me to say that she was going to ride with them this afternoon.'

'I confess, Caroline, that it was rude; but you

know I warned you to expect this kind of thing, and you must determine to have great patience.'

'I could, dear mamma, if it were only Flora's neglect, but I am sure those girls were laughing at me and quizzing me. Both times when they turned away with Flora, they looked at me so mockingly that I could not help feeling vexed with them; and more sorry still that Flora should join in making fun of me.'

'Very likely your imagination has a little to do with that idea, Caroline.'

'No, mamma; if they did not despise me they would ask me to walk with them as well as Flora.'

'It is a different thing, my dear girl; I know that Mrs Staunton was formerly intimate with Lady Seymour, and you know she took Flora with her to call one morning; therefore it is quite natural that the little girls should invite Flora to walk and ride with them; and quite as natural that they should not invite a little girl whose parents are unknown to their mother. Very probably Lady Seymour does not wish her children to associate with others whose families are quite strangers to herself. Do not you think that reasonable? *I* have no acquaintance with Lady Seymour.'

'I did not think of that, mamma. I will allow that it is reasonable that they should not ask me to join them; but they need not laugh at me! I daresay I looked very forlorn, and perhaps cross, "staring at the sea," as Flora said, all by myself; still do not you think it was unkind in them to look so triumphant and so malicious at me?'

'We will charitably hope that nothing of the kind was intended. So now dismiss these little girls altogether from your mind, and let us go to our books.'

CHAPTER VI.

But Caroline had not been mistaken in reading triumph and a little malice in the countenance of Augusta. The first day that Flora had walked with her and her sisters, they had asked if it was her sister with whom they had seen her walking, and Flora had told them how much she loved Caroline, and how they had been constant companions and friends all their lives.

'She looked very grave, I thought,' said Augusta; 'she cannot be half as merry as you are!'

'Oh, she is, sometimes,' replied Flora; 'and she is the steadiest and best girl in the world, and so affectionate. Ah, that was the reason she looked grave. I had been talking so much of you, and wishing to know you so much, that she thought I was rather tired of *her*; and she is so very fond of me that she was sorry.'

'Then I should call her jealous,' said Augusta, 'not affectionate. Why! does she wish to pin you to her side all her life? We shall show her that there are other people whom you can like as well as her.'

'I told her that of course I shall know many others as I become older, and that she must not mind sometimes my being with other girls. But I do not believe I shall love any other as well, at least not for a long time, because I remember her always. I do not recollect any time that she was not my companion and friend; and though I am very glad to come with you sometimes, I always mean to keep my early walk with her. Do you go out early every day?'

Flora was almost saying I must bring Caroline to walk with you, and then you will find how nice and sensible and gentle she is; but she checked herself, as she thought, 'Caroline would not like me to say so, as they have never expressed any wish to know her;' and she was glad she had refrained, when Augusta remarked,—

'Did she not wish to know us as much as you did?'

Flora hesitated; but she was accustomed to speak frankly, so she said, 'No! Augusta; she had not noticed you as much as I did. Her head is full of sea-weeds and actinia and such things just now, and she really feels, I believe, that she wishes for no friend, no intimate companion but myself.'

'Were you not both talking of us the time we passed you so closely on the upper walk? We certainly thought so.'

'Yes; we were. I was admiring you, and wishing to know you, and Caroline allowed that you were very pretty, and beautifully dressed; but she said she was quite satisfied with me, and never should wish to know other girls; and she was a little vexed at my extreme anxiety to become acquainted with you.'

'So she does at least *know* when people are properly dressed. I should not have expected that, to judge from her own extremely common appearance, in her brown Holland jacket and cotton frock. I suppose her parents are poor.'

'Poor!' exclaimed Flora, 'no indeed; on the contrary, Mr Leslie is an extremely rich man, much richer than my father, and Caroline is his only child.'

'How truly ridiculous then of Mrs Leslie to dress her in such a way. Why does she do it?'

'I have heard her say that children's clothes cannot be too simple, as long as they are perfectly neat and clean and well fitting. Those very brown Holland jackets Caroline made herself, on purpose to wear here, that she might go on the shore and seek for weeds and actinia on the rocks, without caring about wetting her sleeves. And it really is much more comfortable: you see I wear just the same sort of clothes, and I never care about them, if I wish to run about, or climb banks, or sit on the grass. And you know I should have to be more careful if I wore such clothes as yours.'

'You are not quite so commonly dressed as Caroline,' said Harriet, the second sister. 'You have a pretty enough muslin frock and cape, and a white hat, but I only see her in that great large brown mushroom, and cotton frocks.'

Flora coloured. 'I must confess,' she said, 'that I put on a little better dress to-day, because I thought I should look so remarkable beside you.'

Augusta laughed. 'That is the advantage of associating with people who know how to dress like ladies. You are immediately desirous to do the same.'

'But surely you think that I and Caroline look as much like ladies in our plain clothes as you do in your smart ones?'

'Well, I will not say precisely that *you* do not look like a lady, and I have scarcely looked at Miss Leslie enough to know. I merely saw what I thought a very common sort of girl.'

'Oh, she does not look common,' exclaimed Flora rather warmly; 'she is not rosy, but her features are beautiful, and her hair like silk, and her eyes so soft and loving. Mamma says that really well-born people always look what they are, in whatever clothes they may be; and no one could mistake Caroline for anything but a very refined, graceful girl.'

'Well, said Augusta, 'we will not dispute about her; don't fire up so; she does not wish to know us, and I don't wish to know her; let us talk of something more interesting.'

And Augusta determined in her own mind that she would punish Caroline for her indifference to herself and sisters, by attracting Flora away from her; and when she succeeded in coaxing her to join them in their early walk, without even sending or making any excuse to Caroline, she could not restrain the triumphant smile that had caught Caroline's eye. She was a clever girl, and could make herself most entertaining when she chose; and she contrived by raillery and flattery to persuade Flora that her old friend had not half appreciated many of her favourite companion's good qualities, and that she should not throw herself away by being intimate with no one else.

Flora was quite unaccustomed to flattery, for Caroline had always been perfectly truthful; and she did not perceive that Augusta was but praising her talents and her conversation and her appearance, in order to gain her desired end of thoroughly vexing and annoying Caroline.

She began to look down on her former friend; and

her conceit grew stronger and stronger. Her heart had given her a twinge of regret when she saw Caroline so sadly seated alone on the bench, but Augusta's mocking words soon chased away the better feeling; and it was without any cloud on her happiness that she joined the riding party in the afternoon.

'What is it to be to-day, Caroline?' asked Mrs Leslie, as she came into the drawing-room dressed for the afternoon walk, and found Caroline poring over the tub of sea-water.

'Mamma, I think I should like to fill my tub now with living creatures; come and see how clear and nice it is, the sea-weeds are quite alive and beautiful, see how brilliant the green laver leaves look in the sunshine. The tide will do, mamma, for the rocks; will you come down?'

'Willingly, dear Caroline; bring your tin, and a paper-knife for taking them off.'

She was soon equipped; as they went under the bridge towards the shore they met Flora and the two eldest of her new friends on ponies; they had taken a canter all along the smooth sand of the bay, and were then pursuing their ride up some of the country roads. Caroline checked her quick step.

'Do not hesitate, dear Caroline, and draw back; speak to Flora, and let her see that you are not out of temper with her,' said her mother.

Caroline made an effort. 'Have you had a pleasant ride, Flora?' she said; 'and are you going home so early?'

'We are not going home,' replied Flora, 'but on some road; and I don't enjoy it much, for this pony is so rough compared with my Snowdrop.'

'Well I wish you a nice ride; I am going to the rocks for actinia; good-bye;' and Caroline walked on after her mother.

'I think,' said Augusta, 'that she does not miss you as much as you supposed; I am sure she looked quite content and satisfied to go groping on those slippery rocks, instead of having a delightful canter as we have been doing.'

'There is no novelty to her in riding,' said Flora; 'because she has at home the most lovely pony you can imagine, and rides often.'

'I suppose she just goes quietly along the road while her mamma walks, you say they are so much together.'

'Mrs Leslie rides with her sometimes, and often she goes long rides with her papa. Oh, she would not care one bit for riding on these hired ponies; and I cannot say I like it much, it is so jolting, and the saddle not comfortable. I think, the next time you ride, I shall go and walk with Caroline.'

'I do not think we shall ride again,' said Augusta; 'for, as you say, the saddles are not nice, and the ponies hard-mouthed and disagreeable. We must drive, and go to see some of the sights in the neighbourhood. There is the Forge Valley, and Brompton Valley, and Oliver's Mount, and so on. You will come with us, of course, Flora?'

'I shall like very much to come with you in the afternoons; but I think in the early morning I really ought to stay with Caroline, she looked so very solitary this morning.'

'But, just now, she seemed quite happy,' remarked Harriet; 'was that her mamma walking with her?'

'Yes; that was Mrs Leslie; oh, she is so kind, Caroline may well look content when she has her mamma to walk with her and to talk to her.'

'Well, she must ask her mamma to come out with her in the morning, as you are otherwise occupied.'

'Oh, but I can; and must spare her my early walk,' said Flora.

Augusta made no answer, but felt determined that she would seize upon Flora the following morning, and so try to punish Caroline a little more for her indifference towards herself and her sisters.

Meantime Caroline and her mother pursued their way across the loose sand towards the shore.

'How much, mamma,' said Caroline, 'I shall enjoy my rides on Selim when we get home again; poor fellow, he has had quite a rest and holiday, has he not?'

'I think Selim would rather be ridden out than spend the whole day in sauntering about the meadow; it is no work, no great exertion I mean, to carry you a few miles.'

'No, indeed; I think he is a very happy little pony; much more so than these poor things that are really overworked, somebody riding them from morning till night; I should not wish to ride on a hired pony. Now, mamma, here we are at the slippery rocks; I mean to look carefully into every pool.'

So she peeped about until she espied a little pink flower on the side of a rock.

'Here, mamma,' she exclaimed, 'I have found one;' and taking the paper-knife she carefully loosened it from the rock. 'Now, I have my first, that is delightful, mamma, let me put it carefully into the can; I remember its long name, it is Actinia Mesembryanthemum.'

Soon Mrs Leslie found a pretty little crab and a small star-fish; Caroline did not much care to take this; but her mamma showed her the curious under side, quite covered with suckers or feelers, each with a wide trumpet-shaped end, so it was also carried off in the can. Then she found a green striped actinia, like the one they had seen in the museum; and also one with a blue bead necklace; and also three or four brown jelly-like lumps that were not unfolded.

'Now, I have six of these pretty kind, mamma, a crab that I hope will prove to be a vanity crab, and a star-fish. I should like very much to find one of the other sort, the kind with the thicker, shorter feelers, and more delicate colours, that one called Bunodes.'

'I think you will scarcely find that sort here, unless we come to a place where there is some flat sand, near the rocks, for they like to get down under the sand. And we had better bring a little spade with us to get them up.'

'Well, mamma, I will find two or three more of some kind, and then we will go home, for I shall be quite anxious to put them out in my tub.'

'We are in good luck, I believe, dear Caroline,' exclaimed Mrs Leslie. 'Come round here; I think this is a Bunodes. See how it is trying to get down among these small pebbles.'

'Oh, mamma, put the paper-knife under; do stop it. See, I will scoop away the stones as fast as possible. Luckily it is rock just below. I have him quite safe, mamma; not bruised or hurt at all. Oh, I am so glad. It is greyish, you see; but he is nearly shut up. Now, shall we go home?'

'Willingly, my dear, if you do not wish to walk further, and we have been loitering about these rocks longer than you would suppose.'

'Yes; we have been out long enough, I think. I

hope the crab and the star-fish will not hurt the actinia whilst they are all jumbled together in this tin. I shall carry it as steadily as possible.'

When they arrived at home, the crab was soon crawling about quite happily at the bottom of the tub, and the star-fish spread himself out nicely, but the actinia refused to take any other appearance but that of a brown lump of jelly. Caroline stuck them upon the largest pebbles, and waited some time hoping to see the flowers unfold.

'You must leave them in peace till to-morrow, dear Caroline; they have not yet forgotten their shaking in the tin, and their forcible separation from their own especial rocks. They will unfold to-morrow, I doubt not.'

'I shall come to see them as soon as I am up, and then I shall hope to find Flora on the bridge.'

But, alas, Flora's resolution was not proof against the persuasions of Augusta, who had hit upon the expedient of going at that hour to a pretty flower and seed shop, saying that the plants looked so much fresher and better, early in the day, before being dusted by many visitors' entrance, and losing their bloom by the heat. So poor Caroline had not even the satisfaction of seeing Flora, though walking with others, and she resolutely paced up and down the terrace for half-an-hour, then she went to examine the plants along the front of the concert room, and then mounting to the top of the garden, she sat on one of the upper benches for some time, admiring the sea and the changing sky, and then she went home.

'No Flora, mamma,' said she; 'I have been quite alone this morning, but I will not think of it. I will do as well as I can till she comes back to me. I am afraid there is no chance of her walking with us this afternoon. I am very sorry for it, mamma.'

'So am I, dear Caroline; but, as you say, we had better not think much about it at present. Flora may send to say that she will be ready for the walk as usual this afternoon.'

With this hope Caroline ran upstairs to look at her red tub, for she had been so eager to meet with Flora in the morning, that she had run out without even remembering the actinia. Now she was much delighted to find that several of them were fully spread out, and the Bunodes was just beginning to show his delicate grey feelers. She could with difficulty leave them to go to her lessons; and as soon as she was at liberty, after dinner, she again went to watch them. But she felt that she wanted some one to sympathise in her pleasure. How much more she should have enjoyed finding these actinia, and attending to them, if Flora had also taken an interest in them. Hitherto they had generally found amusement in the same pursuits, and Caroline soon found her thoughts wandering from the curious creatures before her to brood upon the very unflattering manner in which Flora had deserted her for the company of strangers. Mrs Leslie came into the room without disturbing Caroline from her reverie, and sat watching her for some time. At last she said,—

'My dear little girl, do you not wish to come out this lovely afternoon? I do not like to see you sitting there with that unhappy face. Run for your hat, and let us try whether a fresh sea breeze will not brighten you up!'

Caroline rose and obeyed her mother, but it was evident that she did not take any great pleasure in the proposed walk.

'Where shall we go?' asked Mrs Leslie, as soon as they were out of the house.

'I do not know, mamma,' replied Caroline. 'I do not much care. Down on the sands, or wherever you like.'

'Well, I shall choose for you to-day; we will go on the Castle Hill, where we have never yet been.'

This was rather a long walk; first they had to pass quite through the town, and gradually to mount the slope that forms the neck of the castle promontory. Here they passed through a large and solid gateway, and Caroline began to look about her, and to talk, for their walk hitherto had been accomplished almost in silence.

'Mamma, do look here; what enormously thick walls these are! Are they very old?'

'Yes; they are very old. This castle is supposed to have been built in the time of Stephen. How long ago was that? I daresay you can tell me.'

Caroline considered for a moment.

'It must be more than 700 years old, mamma; but of course I cannot tell exactly, as I do not know the very year in which it was built, and perhaps no one knows the precise time.

'I daresay not. And this very large, solid sort of edifice must have occupied a long time in building. It is astonishing how many of these immensely strong castles, fortified houses, and towns surrounded with walls, were built in the time of our early Norman kings. You know that in those days people were so little restrained by law, or by custom, from all kinds of violence and plunder, that those who had anything to protect, were compelled so to construct their dwellings that they could keep out any one whose entrance was not desirable. It has always seemed to me that their patience and energy must have been very great, to enable them to accomplish these solid masses of masonry.'

'Were many castles then built by the Normans?'

'Indeed there were an immense number; the Romans and Saxons built their castles very much on the same plan as those of the Normans, but they were comparatively few. I have seen it stated that above 1100 castles were constructed in the reign of Stephen alone. Now look, Caroline, at the enormous strength of these walls, even at this great distance of time, and consider that some hundred years ago very few of our modern inventions for lightening labour were in existence. The transport of all these great stones, the hewing into the desired shape, and raising such heavy blocks to their places, must all have been most tedious and difficult work. We make no such durable buildings now, even with the advantage of all our clever appliances of mechanical strength.'

'It does, indeed, mamma, seem quite a puzzle that they could accomplish so much. I suppose they felt quite safe when once shut up within their strong castles. Would a cannon-ball easily batter down such a wall as this? I should imagine that the inhabitants would scarcely even hear the blow!'

'If you thought for a moment, Caroline, you would not make that remark. Do you suppose that the builders of this castle made it strong with the intention that it should resist cannon?'

'Why not, mamma? Do not speak; let me find out what you mean. The builders did not intend it to resist cannon-balls! Oh, now I know. How Flora would have laughed at me. There were no cannon-balls and no gunpowder at the time when this castle was built! Is not that what you were thinking of, mamma?'

'Yes, dear Caroline; and therefore it seems more extraordinary that they should have so toiled to make their fortifications of such great strength, when the only weapons brought against them were arrows, pikes, spears, and so on. They had, indeed, some clumsy and inefficient machines for throwing stones, called balista and catapults, but missiles thrown in that manner could have done but small mischief.'

'And mamma, I remember now that there was no gunpowder till early in the fourteenth century. So the people who came in here for safety must have felt really very secure. I should like to see it all repaired, just as it was at first, and with the same looking soldiers and people living in it.'

'I fear you would think both the people themselves, and their mode of living, but very uncouth and uncomfortable.'

'Oh! but, mamma, just fancy a sentinel of King Stephen's time walking up and down, and peeping through these battlements!'

'He would be, I doubt not, rather a singular object. And now we have come within sight of what remains of the keep! So you may also fancy the governor of the castle living there with his family, perhaps with little daughters like yourself.'

'Did they live in the keep? Is that the name of

this enormous tower? What a pity, mamma, that so much of it has fallen down.'

'It did not fall down, dear Caroline; notice how straight and firm is that solid mass of masonry forming the two sides of the keep that still remain. The other part was battered down by the cannon brought against it during the civil wars between unhappy King Charles and his Parliament.'

'Was the keep built only for the governor to live in then?'

'Oh, no! it was usually divided by three or four floors; you can see the traces of the floors inside those walls; the ground floor or basement was generally filled with arms and stores of all sorts for the use of the garrison, and underneath that was to be found a dungeon for the safe keeping of prisoners. The first floor was partly occupied by private dwelling rooms, in which it is probable that the governor's family, or any guests, were accommodated; and on this floor also were loopholes, and space for soldiers, who could both look out and fire upon any assailants.'

'It was quite a house, mamma.'

'Yes; a sort of house, certainly; above that again were large state rooms, adapted for banquets, or visits of ceremony, but likewise furnished with a gallery and loopholes. Then came an apartment in the roof, which it is supposed was sometimes used as a chapel.'

'And now, mamma, all that remains of this keep is

those two great walls. Do you not think, mamma, that a ruin, though it is picturesque, is also a melancholy looking thing?'

'The ruin of a church I always feel to be a very melancholy thing, whether it fell into disuse from some fierce religious persecution, or, almost more deplorable still, from neglect and want of care. But, dear Caroline, I never regret the ruin of these castles. I always think, "In how much happier times we live."'

'But, mamma, I think it must have been so pleasant to have lived in one of these large castles, with soldiers in armour coming and going, and a minstrel with a harp to sing songs after the dinner; and when the ladies used to embroider banners and scarves for the knights when they went to tournaments.'

'You have a very romantic idea of the whole thing, dear Caroline,' said her mother smiling; 'perhaps it is because the most inviting aspect of the days of chivalry has generally been recorded in all accounts of those times. Now *I* think it far pleasanter to be walking here peacefully, in the nineteenth century, than to be enduring the lives of ladies in the twelfth, thirteenth, or fourteenth.'

'Supposing, mamma, that we were now in the best days of this castle, what should we probably be doing?'

'To begin with our abode, we should inhabit, as a sitting-room, a very small chamber, with stone walls and roof, the floor covered with a kind of litter of rushes, things that at all times have a sickly sort of odour, which could not be improved by the addition of a good deal of dust and dirt. This kind of carpeting, or rather covering for the floor, was in use as late as the time of Henry VIII. The windows in castles were always extremely small, and consequently the supply of fresh air must also have been small. By way of furniture we should have a few oaken stools and chairs; no bookcase, no piano, no vases of beautiful flowers—for the art of gardening was not known, no pictures, and no pretty writing-table; it would have been useless, as but very few knew how to write!'

'All that does not sound so nice as our convenient and pretty drawing-room, mamma?'

'Indeed it does not, and there was nothing else to make up for the want of all our modern advantages.'

'Did they not ride out a great deal, and have hawking parties?'

'When their husbands were at home, and the country in a tolerably peaceful state, they used to partake of the amusement of hawking, and these parties were, I doubt not, very pleasant. But knights who possessed castles were very frequently absent for years, engaged in the wars of the Crusades, or in other warlike expeditions; and as there was no regular post, their wives and families scarcely expected to hear anything about them until their return.

'And during the time of their absence, mamma, the castles at home must have been very quiet and very dull.'

'I should think they were so. Sufficient men were left behind to garrison the castle, and to defend it against any attack: and should any such event occur, the lady of the castle was compelled to take upon herself the task of commanding the soldiers.'

'How glad they must all have been when the knight came home again.'

'There was then a short season of feasting and rejoicing; but gentlemen at that period had absolutely no occupation excepting fighting and the chase, so they soon became weary of a home life, and were off again to attend some tournament, or to join in the petty plundering skirmishes that so often went on among neighbouring landowners, and which were a disgrace to the times.'

'Well, mamma, it could not indeed be a very delightful life, if one considers all these particulars, but still stories about those times are generally very amusing; do you not think so?'

'They are interesting in general, because some very stirring time, or some exciting event, is selected for the subject of the story; and fights with hair-breadth escapes, and brave actions, or desperate misfortunes, are highly amusing to young minds. But you might have a story of the long dreary months during which a lady and her daughter may have pined and watched in vain for some intelligence of father and brothers, with no occupation, and nothing to distract their minds from wearisome anxiety, excepting petty grievances. Of these doubtless they had many, sometimes caused by the rude unruly conduct of the few rough soldiers left to guard them, sometimes by insufficient supplies of their coarse monotonous food, which was often obtained with difficulty, and sometimes they felt an actual want of some incident to vary the dull stagnation of their lives!'

'Oh, mamma, what a picture! Indeed I am much happier as I am; and this blue sea, with the steep cliffs, and this nice short grass to sit on, or to run about on, are still as pleasant to me as they must have been many years since to some poor little girl, who had little else to interest her.'

'Let us sit down on this slope, Caroline, and enjoy the lovely view and the fresh sweet air. It is true that these things are just as fresh and as pleasant as they were to your twelfth-century heroines, and, in fact, we have actually more here to look at. Tell me now what do you see that could not have been seen by a little girl in the time of the Norman kings?'

'First of all, mamma, the Spa bridge was not there, and the concert room, and all that pretty garden was not there. I suppose there was only a rough cliff. And that great row of houses on the top of the south cliff was not there, only a bare field or piece of grass. And all the good-looking houses here have been built not very long since; but I suppose, mamma, that the old town, with the steep streets, was in existence then.

'I doubt whether there is any house in the place as old as these ruins, and even when the castle had stood here for some hundred years, there was only a very small and poor fishing hamlet or village at the foot of the cliff.'

'Then the large old church must have been made when there were scarcely enough people to fill it.'

'Our forefathers did not consider where the people were to come from to fill their large churches. Probably there were very few comers to many of our beautiful cathedrals at the time they were built. You know monasteries were always attached to the churches, and the monks alone must generally have formed the congregation.'

'They liked everything large apparently, mamma; and some of the handsome old church, as well as the castle, is now in ruins. How ugly those little common-looking houses appear beside the ruins.'

'That is now the barracks for a detachment of a few hundred men, which is sent here from the nearest garrison town.'

'Well, this cliff top is a very pleasant place for them to live in. How peaceable now to what it has once been.'

'Yes; these old walls must have seen much of warfare and turbulence. They took their part in most of our civil wars. It was in this stronghold that Piers Gaveston, the—'

'The favourite—the bad favourite, mamma, of unfortunate Edward II.'

'Yes; he shut himself up here, and held out for some time against his indignant foes, but at last his garrison was reduced to starvation. You see, Caroline, if an enemy had possession of the road just outside the first gate, it would be almost impossible to leave the castle or to enter it by any other way.'

'So when they had eaten up all their supplies they could obtain no more?'

'Just so; and they were compelled to surrender. Then the tough old walls underwent two sieges during the war between Charles and his Parliament. It was in the hands of the Royalists, so that will redeem it in your eyes.'

'Yes; that was a better cause than protecting the wretched Gaveston. Well, mamma, what did it do next?'

'It was dismantled and partly pulled down, like many others, by Cromwell's orders. Then it was partially repaired in 1745, that it might be a rock of defence against—'

'Against the Scotch, mamma, and poor Prince Charlie?'

'Yes; but it had not (what would be in your eyes) the sin of actually opposing its walls to your pet hero; and at the close of that rebellion it was suffered to fall into decay, and since that time the old stones have been, bit by bit, tumbling into the sea.'

'And now it is nothing but a pretty addition to the beauty of the place. Well, mamma, I think I do not envy the little girls of Norman times; and as to my vexations about my friends, very likely the friends of those days had the same sort of—, I was going to say unfeelingness, mamma, because I thought only of Flora leaving me, but perhaps I ought to say the same sort of jealousies, for I confess that I have felt very jealous of those Miss Seymours. Do you think, mamma, that my jealousy and selfishness is greater than Flora's fickleness?'

'I do not, dear Caroline, think either of you so very much to blame; it was quite natural that Flora should be attracted as she has been; I only find fault with her for carrying her new enthusiasm too far. And we ought to recollect that the sort of temptation she has had was of a kind peculiarly to suit her disposition.'

'Yes, mamma; so that *I*, who do not generally please strangers, and whom strangers do not please, can scarcely estimate the pleasure that these girls have given her. Is that what you mean?'

'Yes, my dear girl. That is one of the many

instances when we are apt to judge others too much according to ourselves. What does not tempt us, we do not understand should tempt them. And as to your jealousy, what has occurred I well know was especially trying to your very clinging loving nature; and I may say for your comfort, dear Caroline, that you have behaved as well as I could expect. This has been almost your first experience of the fleeting uncertainty of earthly happiness.'

'My first, yes, and I hope, mamma, my last, for a long, long time. I shall try, however, to bring Flora up here before we go back to our homes. I am sure she would have liked our walk to-day. I feel quite sorry to leave this pleasant bank, and to return down through the streets.'

'And I could with pleasure sit here for another hour, gazing on the sea and the beautiful clouds, and feeling the sea breeze, but the daily routine of our lives must be attended to, and so let us make an effort, and set out on our way homewards.'

'Nearly half our time now is over, is it not, mamma. I wonder whether Lady Seymour will be here all the time. I should be so glad if you could walk with me in the mornings also, mamma.'

'To answer that speech all at once, Caroline, I must first tell you that we may probably be here about ten days longer, and that I have heard that Lady Seymour stays for at least six weeks. As to your morning walk, I cannot accompany you at that time, though I am sorry you should be at a loss for a companion. I wish you to have the advantage of the sea air every morning, so you must roam about alone until Flora honours you again with her society.'

'I fear she will not,' said Caroline dolefully, 'if the Miss Seymours are to stay here longer than *we* do.'

'Then you must remember your resolution of this morning, not to annoy yourself about it, but to make the most of this visit to the sea-shore. So do not let Flora spoil all your enjoyment.'

'No, mamma. Where shall we walk to-morrow?'

'We will think of that when to-morrow comes.'

CHAPTER VII.

BUT the next day and the day following were so rainy—in fact, such a determined cloudy sky showed itself—that there was no question of when to walk. Caroline regretted it less than she would have done, because she had now no great delight in her early walk; and in the afternoon she amused herself very well between a book and her red tub.

The second wet day was better still, for in the afternoon, when Caroline was intently watching the movements of the crab, which was actively rushing about between the stones and the sea-weeds, she was surprised and pleased at the entrance of Flora with her mamma.

All her indignant feelings were swallowed up by the stronger one of joy.

'How glad I am to see you, Flora!' she exclaimed, 'Do come and see my actinia; you have never yet seen my tub;' and she drew Flora towards it, after a very hearty embrace.

'That is right, Caroline,' said Mrs Staunton, Flora's mother; 'I really thought that you might be quite vexed with Flora, she has so deserted you lately for her new acquaintances, and I insisted on bringing her here with me to-day, feeling sure you would be at home. I cannot allow you to suppose that it was her own doing in coming now!'

'Oh, I am so sorrow you had to *insist* on her coming to see me!' said Caroline; 'but, indeed, I am too glad to see her any way to feel vexed. Come, Flora, look at my Bunodes and my crab.'

'Oh, really, the weeds look very pretty; how well the green laver looks, and how very clear and nice the water is; but is it not a great trouble to change it?'

'Change it!' it has never been changed yet at all; this is the very first bucket of sea-water that I had; I left the plants two days to fix themselves on the stones, and to recover their move, and now they keep the water fresh and nice; there is no occasion to renew it.'

'And when did you put in these live creatures? How well they all look.'

'I went to get them the day that we passed you going for a ride; but you see I have only two sorts, and one crab, and a star-fish. I mean to try to find several more of different sorts. Do, Flora, arrange an aquarium for yourself, it is so amusing.'

'I am sure it is very amusing, but I do not think I shall manage one during this sea-side visit, for I shall be so much engaged with Miss Seymours; and what will you do with it when we return home? You will have to throw them all away!'

'Oh, no; mamma will manage for me to take them home. I shall have the stones and weeds in a large can filled with sea-water, and I will take the actinia in separate bottles of sea-water, so that they will not jolt about against each other.'

'What a great deal of trouble it will give you, Caroline; I do not think I should have patience; and you see Augusta and Harriet do not care in the least for such things.'

'Augusta and Harriet! Oh, Flora, do you change your own tastes and ways to accommodate yourself to theirs, which, I am sure, are not half so good?'

'Why are you sure? You say that, because they do not happen to care for jelly fish, as if there was nothing in the world worth caring for but them. How prejudiced you are, Caroline, just because you are jealous of those girls.'

'I believe I am a little jealous of them, but I shall try not to be prejudiced. You would have liked collecting weeds and actinia for an aquarium, Flora, if you had not known the Seymours; so, I think you have lost the pleasure of a very amusing and interesting pursuit, and, perhaps, have had nothing instead, excepting discussions on dress.'

'I have had, instead, some very pleasant walks and conversations. Oh! mamma is going; good-bye, Caroline.'

'When shall I see you again, Flora?' asked Caroline.

'Have you made any arrangement for to-morrow, Flora,' asked Mrs Staunton, 'should it prove fine weather?'

'Yes, mamma; you said that I might accept the Seymours' invitation to walk, and ride or drive with them; and, to-morrow we are going to drive to the Forge Valley, I believe; Lady Seymour said she could make room for me.'

'Then, I suppose, you will take your early walk with Caroline?'

'I am not quite sure, mamma; if the Seymours are not out, perhaps I may.'

'Poor Caroline,' said Mrs Leslie, smiling; 'you

put up with her when no one else is to be had. Is it not so, Flora?'

Flora tried to laugh; but Mrs Staunton looked very grave as she kissed Caroline and took leave.

The next morning Caroline came early to her mother's door. 'I am going out, mamma,' she said, 'and I do not in the least expect to see Flora; if I am alone, may I go just below the terrace, and look for some sea-weeds on the bank where the high tide throws them up?' And, having obtained permission, she ran off.

The previous evening her father had been asking her whether she had paid any attention to the zoophytes, commonly so called, or more properly, polypidoms, that are to be found on this and on all sandy coasts. He had told her that they have the appearance of delicate sea-weed or the very finest coral, but are, in reality, the dwellings of minute and beautiful polypi, and are all classified and arranged. So Caroline thought she would look for some, and that the search would prevent her from feeling so lonely in the morning.

'Well, I am glad to see a brighter face,' cried her father, as she entered the breakfast-room; 'a nice run with Flora, I suppose, has given me this pleasure.'

'No, indeed, papa,' replied Caroline, 'I have not even seen Flora at a distance; I waited a long time on the bridge, and then I ran down to the sands and hunted about among the tangled sea-weed, and dry stuff that is on the upper part of the shore; and I picked out these bits, papa,—some of them look like small fishes' bones, and some like very small coral; are any of them polypidoms?'

'Well hunted, indeed, dear Caroline; yes, here are some of the wonderful little dwellings of which I was telling you. These are now quite empty, for the inhabitant soon dries away, when out of the sea, and their home is in the deep sea; these bits are broken up and thrown on shore by the rough waves.'

'Oh, papa, is it then impossible to see them alive?'

'When the fishermen pull up their nets out at sea, these beautiful little things often are brought to light; then they have been immediately placed in a glass filled with sea water, and have been distinctly seen to produce their little pink flower-like heads, at the openings which end these delicate branches, or their feelers, similar to those of your actinia; but unless you can thus examine them immediately, you have no chance of seeing anything but the empty abode.'

'This one, papa, looks quite like a fish's backbone.'

'It does rather so; but look at it through this microscope and you will see that all those little joints are hollow, horny shells, in which the polypus lives.

This one is called sertularia, and that longer one is antennularia; these are, however, but broken and small specimens; if you like to collect some better pieces, I will get you Landsborough's book, which explains to you the whole system of their arrangement.'

'Thank you, dear papa, I should like it very much. Perhaps mamma will go with me this afternoon to find some more actinia, and at the same time I will look for more of these delicate little things.'

So she spent a very pleasant afternoon, though more than once she thought of Flora enjoying the expedition to Forge Valley, and probably never bestowing a regret on her former friend. In the evening she was much amused in sorting and fixing her specimens on paper, and, with the help of her father, in finding out and affixing the correct names.

During the following week she only saw Flora once or twice—the last time she passed her in the garden when walking between Augusta and Harriet, and Flora merely vouchsafed to give her a slight nod of recognition, and passed on without a word. Poor Caroline could scarcely restrain her tears, but she made an effort to meet her father with a cheerful face as she went in to breakfast; and that afternoon Mrs Staunton joined Mrs Leslie and herself as they were going down to the beach.

'My naughty Flora,' said Mrs Staunton, 'is again

enticed away by her new friends; but never mind, Caroline, all things have an end, and so will this violent fancy of hers. I have not interfered with her, because I have an object in letting her take her own way in this instance.'

'Caroline has borne it pretty well,' said Mrs Leslie, 'and her father has very kindly been showing her how to preserve and arrange zoophytes, which has occupied her very pleasantly. I suppose, Caroline, you are longing to commence your daily search?'

'Oh, yes, mamma; I will hunt about whilst you and Mrs Staunton walk.' And she diligently pursued her investigation of the dirty-looking heaps of weed, every now and then running after her mother to show her some wonderful beauty.

'That one, Caroline,' said Mrs Staunton, 'is surely a sea-weed—is it not?' as Caroline brought a bunch of delicate, white-looking leaves growing thickly on one root.

'I do not know; it is not at all like any of the other zoophytes; there is plenty of this same thing coloured brown, and I have always taken it for a sea-weed, and never took it in to papa, but this white bunch is so pretty, that I will take it. I have found one or two different sorts to-day, mamma.'

'Then to-morrow or Monday must complete your collection for this time, dear Caroline, as papa wishes to return home on Tuesday.'

'And you, Mrs Staunton,' asked Caroline, 'do you also go back on Tuesday?'

'No; I think we shall remain till the end of the week.'

'I shall be very glad to be at home again,' said Caroline. 'I hope Flora will feel happy to come back to her old life; do you think she will?'

'I trust so, my dear girl, and I half expect Flora will have a lesson on the score of her fickleness before we leave Scarborough; but I cannot explain to you yet. Do you intend to come to the shore again to-morrow.'

'I do, indeed; unless mamma wishes to go elsewhere,' replied Caroline.

'No; I quite intended to devote myself to you, Caroline, whilst we were here; so I shall go where you please. Now for home, my dear Caroline.' And she was soon busy by her father's side sorting her specimens.

'Look, papa, is this pretty white bunch of leaves only a sea-weed? I am afraid so, and though they are pretty, I do not find them nearly so interesting as the polypidoms.'

'But, Caroline, this one is a very beautiful polypidom—it is a flustra; you must fetch the microscope and look at it carefully. You will see all over the flat leaf little cells, more resembling the cells in a beehive than anything else, and in each of those cells a creature *has* lived.'

'Oh, papa, it is very beautiful; how minute and yet how distinct are the little cells.'

'This kind is called Flustra carbasea; it has only cells on one side of the leaf, and has that particularly shining, transparent look. There are other flustras, larger and darker, which have the cells on both sides of the leaf.'

'Ah, then, those I have frequently seen, and I stupidly thought they were common sea-weeds, but I will get some of them to-morrow.'

'The others are Flustra foliacea; it grows in long jagged leaves, with rounded ends; and there is another called Flustra truncata, because it looks as if the ends of the leaves had been snipped off. Try to find both of those.'

This, Caroline accomplished before breakfast on the Saturday, and she had been so busy during the week, that her father thought she must have collected nearly all the kinds that are met with on that coast. He agreed to look them all over with her in the evening, and when she and her mother set out in the afternoon, she was bent on finding at least five more kinds during their walk. On the bridge they found Mrs Staunton.

'Let us walk up and down the bridge for a time,' she said. 'I am watching for Flora; she is gone out to ride with the Seymours, but as I know they have some of their London friends with them, I rather wish to see what will occur.'

Presently they saw Flora come gently down the road on the pony that she had before ridden, and after looking all round, she went forward on the sands, now and then looking back, and evidently in search of her friends.

'Why did they not come to fetch her?' asked Caroline; 'it must be so disagreeable to be riding all alone.'

'I rather imagine that they have forgotten Flora, and have gone out to ride without her,' said Mrs Staunton; 'and I am earnestly hoping that such is the case.'

Caroline looked surprised. 'Oh, Mrs Staunton,' she said, 'are you really meaning what you say? Do you like Flora to be so rudely neglected?'

'I think, dear Caroline, that were she to receive from others the same sort of indifference with which she has treated you, it might make her a little conscious of her own fickle and unfeeling conduct.'

'There are some ladies riding,' said Caroline, pointing to the sands near the harbour; 'but there are four, not two; still I think that the two nearest are the Miss Seymours.' And she watched them as they cantered rapidly towards the bridge. Flora meantime had turned again to mount the hill, not having perceived her friends in the distance, and was slowly coming across the soft sand. At other times when she had ridden with Augusta and Harriet, they had come round on their ponies to the house where Mrs Staunton lodged, and having arranged to do so again, Flora had waited for them, and at last, becoming impatient, had mounted and gone round to the Crescent, but hearing there that they had already started, she rather pettishly took the way to the sands, as they usually commenced their ride by a canter along the edge of the bay. Flora was the more annoyed at not finding them, for she had expected to meet with some of their London friends, who had come to Scarborough a few days previously. Augusta had been loud in her praises of the beauty and cleverness of the two Miss Montagues, who learnt to dance from the same fashionable mistress, and had the same music and Italian masters. And now a very disagreeable suspicion shot across Flora's mind, that her new friends were not perhaps so eager for her society as they had been, when no more fashionable acquaintances were at hand. She was roused from her musing fit by the sound of horses' feet behind her, and turning, she saw Augusta and Harriet. 'Oh! here you are,' she exclaimed, 'I could not think what had become of you.'

'You see,' said Augusta, 'that we have our friends, Miss Montagues, with us, and we have settled to take a long ride in the country, so we cannot stay on the sands with you to-day—Good-bye;' and switching her pony she cantered past Flora, followed by her sister and their two companions, handsome girls, apparently about the same age as themselves.

Caroline, Mrs Leslie, and Mrs Staunton witnessed this encounter from the bridge above. They could not, it is true, hear the words that passed, but they could see first the pleased surprise of Flora, the haughty air with which Augusta shook her off, the patronising nod from Harriet, and the cool indifference of the two strangers; and then they marked the indignant flush which overspread Flora's face, as she struck the pony sharply after a moment's pause, and made the animal dart up the hill towards her own home.

'Oh! poor Flora,' exclaimed Caroline; 'how excessively rude and disagreeable in the Miss Seymours to leave her in that manner, after all the pains they have taken to engage her always to be with them. Do let us go, mamma, and ask if she will come to walk with us!'

'No, my dear little forgiving girl, I must beg that you will not take any notice of Flora to-day. She does not know that we have been watching her, and she knows that you and your mother are certainly gone out for your walk by this time. She does not deserve any comfort at present; leave her to think over the conduct of her new friends, and to compare it with her own conduct to yourself. I only hope her conscience may be true enough to compare them at all.'

'I cannot bear to go on with my walk whilst I know that poor Flora is alone in the house, perhaps crying, and feeling herself left and slighted. Pray, Mrs Staunton, allow me to run and beg her to come and assist in my search.'

'No, my dear, I cannot grant your request; it would spoil all the possible effect of what has just occurred.'

'Well, then, I must go alone, I suppose, and hunt in what you called the other day my dirt heaps, whilst you and mamma walk.' They pursued their way down to the sands, but Caroline could not feel the same interest in her pursuit, and after finding three or four specimens, she sauntered after her mother, not even attempting to join in the conversation between her and Mrs Staunton.

After they had gone home, Caroline's father sat waiting for her to bring her specimens as usual, and at last he asked, 'Have you nothing to show me to-day, Caroline? I thought you went out with the intention of bringing back every possible zoophyte that has ever visited these shores. What has occurred so to change the course of your ideas?'

Caroline related to her father what had passed, and added that she had felt so much grieved for Flora's evident distress at the abandonment of her friends, that she had not searched for her curiosities so eagerly and successfully as usual. 'But, papa, I have some bits which are new to me, one in particular that is very pretty,' and she exhibited a little bit of Crisia Eburnea. 'I am quite sure that it *is* a zoophyte,' she said; 'I know now how to distinguish them from seaweeds, I think. Is it not a good specimen?'

'It is a good piece, and of a kind not very common on this coast. Indeed, I think you have done very well this afternoon, in spite of the disturbance of your equanimity. What else have you?'

'A bit, a very small bit, of the long pipe-like sort that you were describing to me.'

'Yes! Tubularia indivisa; and now, Caroline, I really think you have a very fair beginning for your little collection. When we get home we will pursue this kind of study as far as books will take us, apart from the actual visible things themselves.'

'And then, papa, we shall look forward with much more pleasure to our next visit to the sea-shore. Will you look over all I have now, and see if I have added the names correctly?'

'With pleasure, dear Caroline; we will look at the description of each in Landsborough as we go on.'

'Well, then, here is my very first specimen, Sertularia Abietina, and my three sorts of Flustras; and this is a bottle-brush; what is the name, papa?'

'Thuiaria Thuja; that is common everywhere, but pretty and curious.'

'Then my greatest beauty, Salicornia, and also Crisia Eburnea; both so delicate and **pretty**.'

'They are both rather rare on this coast; yet I admire almost more the bit now in your hand, the Sea Cypress, or Sertularia Cupressina, it is so extremely graceful!'

'Oh! but this next one is really the prettiest of all, Sertularia operculata, or Sea hair. I can scarcely conceive, dear papa, that every little minute joint has contained a living creature; such an airy-looking mass of mere threads!'

'It is, indeed, a marvellous creation!'

'Then, papa, I have Thuiaria Articulata, not so pretty as many others; Cellularia Reptans, that is small and beautiful; and last of all, the curious parasite that grows over something else, Membranipora pilosa. Oh, no, here is one more, and a pretty one, Antennularia Antennina. I suppose, papa, called so from its resemblance to the antennæ of insects?'

'Yes, my dear; they are very nicely preserved, and neatly named. Was not this study better than objectless reveries over the silly conduct of your companion, dear Caroline? Remember that occupation and the study of something is always the best remedy for annoyances that are thrown upon us by others. I mean annoyances that have not arisen through any negligence or fault of our own; the remedy for *such* self-caused troubles, is to repair the wrong earnestly and perseveringly; this grief of yours was of the passive sort that you could not help; but had only to endure.'

'I understand, papa; it did me no good at all to think about Flora, and lament her absence; and it made no difference at all in her feelings towards me; so it was best to think about it as little as I could, and to interest myself with something else.'

'Just so; recollect this for your next trouble, whenever it may come; if you can remedy the evil, do so at once; and if not, bear it patiently, and occupy yourself incessantly.'

'I shall be very much occupied on Monday, papa; I shall have my aquarium to pack, and my zoophytes; besides all the usual packing of lesson books and music, and clothes.'

'All the better, dear Caroline; we shall start very early on Tuesday, so pack all on Monday.'

CHAPTER VIII.

CAROLINE had some doubts about going out for the early walk on Monday; she thought that Flora would scarcely walk again with the Miss Seymours after their rudeness to her; and still she might not like so immediately to fall back on her old friend, and so confess how evanescent had been the professed love of Augusta and Harriet; and she thought that she should really feel very awkward for Flora at their first meeting. On the other hand, if she did not go out, and Flora should be waiting for her on the bridge, intending to talk to her of all that had passed, and to say something of sorrow for her desertion, how sulky and unforgiving would it appear not to be there to welcome her! So, at last, Caroline determined to go out as usual, to linger a little on the bridge, and then, should no Flora appear, to pursue her walk alone. There was to be no walk on Monday afternoon, which she meant to employ in preparing her treasures.

When Caroline left the house for her last walk by the shore, she felt that she should quite regret the lovely morning air, especially on those days when the sea was quiet and the sky unclouded. 'It is really rather strange,' she thought, 'that I should have liked this place so much, after all; I shall not be afraid of leaving home again, for I see that new things and new ideas can even prevent one from feeling a sorrow so much as one would do at home, in accustomed places. Oh, how happy I shall be if Flora comes to me again this morning!'

She loitered long on the bridge, till her hope died away; and then she went down on the sand, and walked to and fro quietly, until she thought her usual time out of doors had passed.

Flora, on her part, had had many debates with herself, whether or not to go out to meet Caroline. She was not aware that the scene on the sands had been witnessed by any one, and she shrunk from the shame of acknowledging how much mistaken she had been in Augusta and Harriet. Then it seemed so cowardly to run back immediately to Caroline, as if she could not bear to be alone; and she rather dreaded that the Seymours should again see her with Caroline, for though she felt their conduct to be despicable, she had not the courage to feel indifferent to their ridicule. So she stayed at home, blaming her friends, blaming herself, and half angry with poor Caroline, because she had done nothing amiss in the matter; on the contrary, had shown her judgment to be the best of the two.

At luncheon, Mrs. Staunton asked if Flora had walked with Caroline in the morning; and on receiving a reply in the negative, she expressed some surprise, adding,—'I should have thought, Flora, that the very unkind and rude conduct of your new friends yesterday, would have shown you how truly inferior they are to the steady and warm-hearted companion of your life; and that you would have had the sincerity at once to have gone to Caroline, and begged her to forgive and overlook your behaviour to her, and to allow you again to be her friend!'

Only one part of what her mother said attracted Flora's attention.

'Their unkind and rude conduct, mamma—how did you know? Who told you of it?'

'My own eyes, Flora. Mrs. Leslie and I were on the Spa bridge with Caroline; we saw you go to the shore on your pony, evidently looking for those who had forgotten you, and then we saw them come up to you, and when they observed your intention to join them, we saw them carelessly take leave of you, as much as to say, now we have better companions, we do not want you! Certainly we did not hear the words that passed, but I am sure they must have been of cutting coldness, to judge from your indignant ascent of the hill on your way home!'

Flora coloured with vexation.

'Then Mrs. Leslie and Caroline also saw me left there? Oh, how I wish we had never come to this nasty Scarborough! Caroline will so triumph over me, for she said at first that the Seymours looked haughty and conceited; and now she has seen them treat me with scorn. How glad she must have felt at witnessing my discomfiture.'

'I am sure that Caroline has no such feelings; she expressed the utmost sympathy with you, and indignation against them; and she begged me to allow her to come here for you, that you might not feel yourself neglected and left by all! I would not

K

hear of her doing so, because I wished you to suffer what you had inflicted on her. But you scarcely seem to think that you have treated her ill.'

'Did she, indeed, seem to feel sorry that I was so treated? Do you think she has been much annoyed herself by my leaving her as I have done?'

'She has felt it extremely. Mrs Leslie told me that she had previously no idea that Caroline's love for you was so strong; and, far from blaming you, she has supposed that her own dulness and inferiority to others was the reason that you could not be content with her society. Indeed, she is a generous and a humble-minded girl. I wish I could see you more like her in many respects.'

'And do you think then, mamma, that she would be glad to be with me again, as we used to be?'

'I am not only sure of that, but I am sure that not one reproach will ever be spoken by her. But I do hope that you will reproach yourself.'

'To-morrow morning, mamma, I will go on the bridge as I used to do, and if Caroline comes, I will tell her that I am sorry I neglected her.'

Mrs. Staunton did not tell Flora that Caroline would have left Scarborough on her way home before the usual time for their meeting on the bridge, because she thought that Flora had scarcely been mortified enough to make her sensible of her own bad conduct; and she thought a little doubt as to

Caroline's feeling towards her would perhaps have good effect.

During the afternoon of Monday, Caroline was busily employed, first of all in packing carefully her specimens of polypidoms, then in transferring her actinia into a number of wide-mouthed bottles filled with sea water. These were then placed in a wide hamper which was to travel on the floor of the carriage, so that Caroline could watch that none of the bottles were upset. The stones and sea-weeds attached were put pretty closely together in a large tin vessel with a lid, and the sea water contained in that and in all the bottles, Caroline thought would be quite sufficient to supply a tub similar to that she had had at Scarborough. This was to be found at home, as the original red tub was by far too heavy an article to travel conveniently. During her arrangements, Caroline listened eagerly every time the door-bell rang, hoping that Flora would come to say good-bye to her, but the afternoon passed, and evening came, tea time, and candle-light time, and no Flora.

'Oh, mamma,' said Caroline, pitifully, 'I really did think that she would have come in to-day to see us before we left. Do you think it possible that she went again to walk with the Seymours? Even if she did, there has been time since for her to come. I begin to be afraid, mamma, that she will never love me again,' and Caroline burst into tears.

'If Flora were to feel that doubt about you, Caroline, it would be more suitable. You have done nothing to alienate her affection; but she *has* done what might disgust one less strongly attached than you. I have not the slightest doubt that Flora will be glad and thankful to be allowed to love you again. But you must yet have patience a little longer. They do not return home for the next ten days, and I expect that Flora will meet with many mortifications during that time, which I trust will send her home with a little more sense than she has shown lately.'

'I wish the ten days were over, mamma. I do not wish her to be mortified, and I shall be so glad to see her back. Would you like me to go to their house just to say good-bye to her?'

'No, Caroline, I think not; go to bed, for we shall be up early.'

By the time that Flora went slowly to the bridge, revolving in her mind how she should speak to Caroline, the Leslie family, the actinia in their bottles, and the sea-weeds in their large tin jar, were far on the road towards their home. Flora was rather relieved at first at not finding Caroline, for a night's reflection had made her feel a little ashamed of her own conduct, especially as events had shown how very much misplaced had been her sudden and violent admiration of Augusta and Harriet Seymour.

But when a quarter of an hour or twenty minutes passed, she began to feel uneasy, and to ask herself how it would be should Caroline indeed not wish to resume their intimacy. Her mamma, it is true, had described Caroline's behaviour the day they had watched the riding party from the bridge, but two whole days had passed since, and Caroline might now think, that as Flora had not come near her, neither would *she* seek one that apparently had no love left for her. With no very light heart she was turning to go home, when she met, face to face, Augusta, Harriet, their younger sister, and the two Miss Montagues. Augusta, who was first put on a condescending smile.

'Well, Flora,' she said, 'I suppose you are waiting for your old companion, Miss Leslie?' and slightly nodding, she passed on with her party. Flora's indignation was strong enough to prevent her from crying, and she went home with a firm step.

'Mamma!' she said, 'I have been out to meet Caroline, but she is holding back from *me* now, for she did not come on the bridge at all.'

'There is a better reason than that for your not seeing her; she must be now more than half way towards home.'

'Home!' exclaimed Flora; 'have they left Scarborough? Gone away quite?'

'Yes! their intended three weeks here came to

an end to-day. You knew that they only thought
of staying for that time; did you not?'

'I heard so at first, but I had forgotten all about
the time. It is rather hard, mamma, that just when
I had determined to try to make amends to Caroline,
I find I have not the power.'

'That shows you that we cannot choose our own
times for behaving well; we carelessly let the opportunity slip, and another never may come!'

'How much longer shall *we* stay then, mamma?'

'Ten days, or perhaps a fortnight.'

'Oh, dear! I am so sorry. I shall not in the
least enjoy it now; I wish we could go home to-day!'

'Then you acknowledge that the presence of
your admired friends Augusta and Harriet is now no
attraction to you!'

'You know, mamma, that they left me the other
day, and again this morning I saw them on the bridge,
and they passed me by, and said they supposed I
was waiting for my old companion. I will never go
out of the house again whilst we stay here. I cannot
bear it!'

'I shall not allow you to give up your daily walks,
Flora. If you have brought on yourself the vexation
of being slighted by these girls, you must bear it as
well as you can, and consider that you slighted
Caroline in the same way, although you had seemed

to love her all your life. So your conduct was far worse than theirs towards you. They have only known you a very short time, and cannot think very highly of you after seeing the way in which you deserted your own friend!'

Every day Flora regretted more and more the absence of Caroline. Her morning walks were solitary and wearisome, and though in the afternoon her mother took her with her either to drive or to walk, and once or twice for a short row along the coast, yet she terribly missed the quiet cheerfulness that had formerly made so pleasant a contrast to her own wild spirits. She tried to amuse herself by making an aquarium like Caroline's, and by collecting pebbles on the shore, but want of some one to sympathise in her success or failure, took away all interest in those pursuits. As to the two Seymours, it was worse than if they had altogether left Scarborough, for by degrees they discontinued even the few words with which they had greeted her, and a very indifferent nod, as they passed her in walking or driving, was but an aggravation of her annoyance. Mrs Staunton left her very much to herself, and the days appeared to her longer than she had ever known them. As, however, all things, whether pleasant or otherwise, come to an end, the week gradually wore on, and Flora with much satisfaction heard her mother give directions about their journey home on the following Tuesday. Her actinia had all failed in consequence of her hurry in putting them into the tub before the weeds were settled sufficiently to preserve the water, so, with the exception of a few pebbles, she had no addition to her preparation for the journey, and very joyfully took her place in the carriage and bade good-bye to Scarborough. When they had gone a few miles, however, she began to anticipate what would be her welcome from Caroline, and she felt that even in her own pleasant home she should feel but little happiness, if Caroline were estranged from her. She sat silently thinking over this, till her mother said,—'Why, Flora, I was hoping to see your face brighten a little as we drew near home. You have been so desirous to leave Scarborough that I really thought you would be pleased when the time came, but here is a most dismal face indeed. What am I to understand—do you neither like to go home nor to stay away?'

'I am so afraid, mamma, about what Caroline will be when I see her again. If she were to speak to me, or nod at me, as the Seymours did, I should be almost ready to kill myself. I do not know what I should do.'

'I am glad that your conscience tells you that you deserve some such treatment; and, pray, observe also how much pleasure you have marred by your folly. First of all, you have disappointed me, independently of the vexation of seeing that I have so silly a child.'

'Disappointed you! How, mamma?'

'My object in coming to Scarborough has been unfulfilled. When Mrs Leslie told me that she should like to take Caroline to the seaside for a time, I agreed to go also, thinking that it would be a nice variation for you, and that both you and Caroline would enjoy it more together. Now, as I am not fond of the sea-shore myself, and like to be at home in the summer months, I gave up my own comfort to minister to yours; and had I given pleasure by so doing, I should not have regretted it. But I have pleased nobody. You only caused sorrow to Caroline, you have brought sorrow and discomfort on yourself, and you have shown me that my daughter has far less sense than I thought she had.'

'Oh, mamma, I had no idea I had done so much harm as that. I am sorry—very sorry.'

'Then you have spoilt Caroline's time here very completely, for though she tried hard to amuse herself and make the best of it, I am sure that no day passed without a heartache on your account.'

The tears came to Flora's eyes. 'Poor Caroline, I am sure she deserved better treatment from me. I will, indeed, mamma, try to make amends to her by loving her more than ever.'

'If she will let you, that is. And for yourself,

Flora, I need not ask whether you have had much real enjoyment since we left home. Even when the Seymours appeared to think much of you, you must have had a consciousness of wrong conduct that could not have left you free to be happy.'

'I have, indeed, done more harm than I thought of. But what can I do now, mamma? Unluckily we cannot begin again at the day I first saw the Seymours.'

'If Caroline should be cold towards you, you must bear it patiently and affectionately, and keep in your memory how well your love merited indifference from her. My only fear is that you will too soon forget all that has passed during the last three weeks.'

'I will not, mamma. You will see how steady I shall be. I will go down to our little gate to-morrow morning, and if Caroline does not come also, I will go in and beg her to forgive me.'

Full of this intention, Flora went to bed more happily. Her home looked fresh and beautiful; the trees in such full leaf, the flower garden brilliant, the rooms so large and luxurious, after the poorly furnished lodging. But Flora was too full of the meeting on the morrow to be much occupied with such things.

Caroline had passed a quiet pleasant week, having resumed all her old occupations and amusements. She had determined that on the morning following Flora's arrival at home, she would, as she had often done formerly, hang out a signal flag from her window, which would at once show Flora that she hoped to resume their former habits immediately, and that she meant to say nothing about the past estrangement.

Flora had not thought about the flags, so she started with joy when, on opening her window and leaning out to feel the soft pure air, she perceived the fluttering little flag above the trees.

'Dear Caroline,' she thought, 'she means to be just as usual. Blue! that is to say, "Will you come into our garden?" unless, indeed, it is by chance that the flag is hung out.' She ran down to her mother's room. 'Oh, mamma!' she exclaimed, 'the blue flag is out! You know that asks me to come. Do you think she has really just put it out, or only left it there by chance, not meaning it for me?'

'You had better take it in its best sense, Flora, and accept the invitation at once.'

Away flew Flora across the park and in at the little gate, then along the path to Caroline's own little garden. There stood Caroline, and Flora flung herself into her arms. 'You saw my flag then, Flora? I was afraid you might not wish to come; but I am so glad to see you.' Flora could only cry. 'Oh, Flora, what is the matter?' continued Caroline; 'our first morning at home again, try to feel happy.'

'*You* may well feel happy,' said Flora, 'for you have done no harm. But I do not know when I shall be right again; not, at any rate, till you say you have quite forgiven me, and will love me again.'

'I never left off loving you,' said Caroline, 'and I did not mean to say a word about anything that is gone by, but to be always your real and own friend, as I hope you will be to me;' and a warm kiss sealed the bargain.

THE END.

COLSTON AND COY, PRINTERS, EDINBURGH.

www.ingramcontent.com/pod-product-compliance
Lightning Source LLC
Chambersburg PA
CBHW030315170426
43202CB00009B/1011